Dr. John Coleman

ABORTION: GENOCIDE IN AMERICA
The most vitally important issue in U.S. history

The Nation's Leadership Fails Litmus Test on Abortion

ⒸMNIA VERITAS®

John Coleman

John Coleman is a British author and former member of the Secret Intelligence Service. Coleman has produced various analyses of the Club of Rome, the Giorgio Cini Foundation, Forbes Global 2000, the Interreligious Peace Colloquium, the Tavistock Institute, the Black Nobility and other organisations with New World Order themes.

ABORTION: GENOCIDE IN AMERICA
The most vitally important issue in U.S. history

The Nation's Leadership Fails Litmus Test on Abortion

© Omnia Veritas Ltd - 2023

⊘MNIA VERITAS®

www.omnia-veritas.com

I n this scholarly work by Dr. Coleman, he explains in detail why notwithstanding Roe vs. Wade, abortion in the United States remains unconstitutional and unlawful. The leading cause of death in the U.S. is not what the American Medical Association (AMA) says it is, but rather, it is infanticide, known as abortion, which the AMA does not bother to list in its annual statistics.

After searching 37,000 pages of the Annals of Congress, the Congressional Globe and the Congressional Record, the author says he was not able to find anything in the Constitution that would legalize abortion. Dr. Coleman cites the late Senator Sam Ervin, a great constitutionalist as saying: In Roe vs. Wade, the Supreme Court found a power in the U.S. Constitution that does not exist. The leading threats to the maintenance and stability of our Republican form of government and our rights guaranteed by the Bill of Rights are abortion and gun control in that order, says Dr. Coleman. The Supreme Court justices who voted for abortion, acted outside the pale and the ken of the Constitution. Abortion is a product of so-called 'free love' which now permeates every corner of the United States. Women are murdering their babies at an alarming rate, and this unholy state of affairs must be halted, even if a second American Revolution has to be fought to put an end to it, the author says.

This book is recommended to every person who has any regard for the Constitution and Dr. Coleman believes that relentless opposition to abortion must be forcibly expressed until Congress overturns Roe vs. Wade, which it has the power to do, even by a majority of one single vote.

HN COLEMAN

12 |

1

THE LEADING CAUSE
OF DEATH IN AMERICA

The leading cause of death in America is not what the American Medical Association (AMA) says it is, but infanticide, known as abortion, which the AMA does not even bother to include in its annual statistics.

After searching 37,000 pages of The Annals of Congress, The Congressional Globe and Congressional Record, a task I began in 1971, and after having spent five years of intensive study of the U.S. Constitution, I can say that there is no power for abortion found in the U.S. Constitution.

For a measure to be constitutional, it must first be studied to see if such a power already exists in the U.S. Constitution, that is to say expressed or expressly implied, or in consonance with or pursuant to an existing power. If no such power is found, then the measure falls to the ground and it cannot be taken.

As Senator Sam Ervin told me:

> In Roe vs. Wade, the Supreme Court found a power in the U.S. Constitution that does not exist.

The leaders of conservatism and defenders of the Constitution and the Bill of Rights, bowing to pressure from Henry Hyde, Newt Gingrich, Jim Nicholson and Richard

Riordin, the delegates to the Republican Party National Committee Convention, held at Palm Springs in January of 1998, voted against the courageous resolution submitted by Tim Lambert, chairman of the Texas Home Schooling Coalition and backed by the Christian Coalition.

Lambert's resolution was for the Republican Party to cut off funding for candidates who would not support a ban on "late term 7 abortions," the gruesome ritual murder of children, who are wrenched from the mother's womb, their heads crushed and their brains sucked out. Those of the party hierarchy with an eye to the upcoming elections, who regarded the collection of filthy lucre of greater importance than ending the cruel, horrifying murder of helpless infants, used all manner of rhetoric to persuade delegates not to split the party. The most compelling assertion came from Rep. Henry Hyde:

> There is no reason I am in Congress other than to fight for the unborn child. The worst thing you can do for the pro-life movement is for us to lose our majority. We need people to pass laws... we need converts... If you read these people out of the party they will never come over to our side.

As is well known to *World In Review* subscribers, Henry Hyde helped to pass "laws" that were absolutely unconstitutional, such as HR1710, HR2580, not to mention his almost jocular attitude toward Waco. If Hyde was an example of the kind of people the Republican Party wished to keep as leaders, then those who value principle above expediency should form their own party. As for "new converts" (and many long-time members), how many of them who do not oppose child murder, can be counted upon to vote for true conservative measures when the chips are down?

And when the big push comes to utterly destroy the people's 2nd Amendment rights, how many of these "new converts" and "moderates" in the party will stand up and be counted on the side of defending the Constitution and the Bill of Rights?

The question is self-evident: Will they desert the people in droves for the sake of the expediency, or will they uphold their oath of office? If experience is anything to go by, don't count on the "moderates" in the Republican Party to do the right thing.

How sad that the leadership of the Republican Party of today has fallen into a slough; they wobble around and if we compare them 8 with Congressmen of the period 1880-1900, it is hard to believe just how far in quality the representatives of the people have fallen. Randy Tate, director of the Christian Coalition, put it in perspective when he said: "We had hoped that the Republican Party would lead, but if they will not, then we invite them to follow as we take the lead."

Former Speaker of the House, Newt Gingrich, talked of a "tactical mistake" if the resolution not to fund those who favor child murder were carried. What kind of a leader is this when what was at stake - condoning or opposing child murder - could be described in terms of "tactics?" In my opinion, the major problem with the Republican Party is that with a few notable exceptions, it is bereft of men of true leadership. Instead the party is top-heavy with hierarchy-politicians more concerned with their own welfare and the pursuit of success, than with principles, especially the principle of upholding and defending the Constitution and the Bill of Rights.

The two greatest threats to the maintenance and stability of our Republican form of government and our rights guaranteed by the Bill of Rights are abortion and gun control. The Supreme Court justices who voted for abortion acted outside the pale and ken of the Constitution when they said the 4th Amendment Right to Privacy; that "right" could be interpreted as "rights" of a woman to abort her unborn child.

In my five years of study at the British Museum in London - which included a study of ancient nations and their cultures — I never found a nation among them that willingly permitted the mass-murder of their children. In fact, even the Egyptian and Babylonian priesthood did not practice mass-murder of children; they murdered only selected victims for ritual sacrificial purposes.

The priesthood of those nations could do this because of their power and wealth arising from their alleged "higher secret knowledge." The people of Egypt did not dare to disobey the priest-rulers until the reign of Amenhotep IV in the Eighteenth Dynasty. It is utterly beyond explanation why the American people allow the liberal "priest class" and the politicos they control, along with the "priests" of the Supreme Court with their alleged "higher knowledge" of the Constitution, to go on murdering children at the rate of 1.4 million a year for reasons of being inconvenient to take responsibility for sexual unions, the "free love" doctrine of Madame Kollontei, (1872-1952) the Bolshevik commissar who toured the U.S. in the 1920s preaching the doctrine of sex without responsibility.

"Free love" is a drug permeating every corner of our nation and it has now got an entire generation of women hooked. While in this mentally-drugged mind-controlled induced state, women are murdering their own unborn infants at a staggering rate. This unholy state of affairs is unconscionable and must be halted, even if it means we have to fight a Second American Revolution to put an end to the savagery.

As I hope to demonstrate, abortion is unconstitutional, and we must stand fast on the Constitution and the Bill of Rights as the highest law of the land. We must wage relentless opposition by whatever means possible under the law, against those who are violating it. Kollontei's book, *The Origin of the Family*, is a sharp attack on the sanctity of marriage and the family. It is the handbook of the so-called women's rights movement in America, although most protagonists of the movement have probably heard of it. Supreme Court justices are not immune from political influence and it seems to me that political pressure was behind the passing of Roe vs. Wade. It is a flaw in our system whereby Supreme Court justices are proposed by the president, and it goes without saying that the political beliefs of the president must undoubtedly influence his choice.

2

THE CONSTITUTION IS IMMUTABLE

The great thing to remember is that the Constitution cannot be fragmented nor can its clauses be isolated. The Constitution has to be seen as a whole; otherwise its perfect equipoise is lost.

There is absolutely no connection between the 4th Amendment right to privacy and abortion "rights."

The 9th Amendment was written as a restriction upon the Federal Government to stop them reading their predilections between the lines of the Constitution. The 9th Amendment clearly voids any pretended connection between abortion "rights" and the 4th Amendment. The 9th Amendment voided the old rule of law.

Another point I wish to interpose here: A nine-judge Supreme Court cannot possibly meet the needs of a country the size of the United States.

We need at least fifty such judges on the Supreme Court, and I venture to suggest that if there were more justices when Roe vs. Wade was ruled on by the court, instead of being submitted as a constitutional amendment, it would have been referred to the legislative branch immediately, where it rightly belongs.

The abortion issue is a matter for the people of the U.S. to decide and this can only be done through an amendment to the Constitution ratified by all of the states.

The bottom line is that the Supreme Court acted as legislators in Roe vs. Wade, and no court in the land has the power to do so.

Moreover such justices ought to be elected by the people of each state and not by the President, even if such appointments are supposed to be confirmed by the Senate.

The Supreme Court as presently constituted does not represent the American people.

The Constitution does not mean what the Supreme Court says it means. The Supreme Court made abortion the law although the power of abortion is not mentioned anywhere in the Constitution and the Bill of Rights, nor is it in consonance with existing power (already in the Constitution), nor is abortion expressly implied. Abortion is a prohibition and can never be the law of the land.

Nor could Justice Rehnquist and his colleagues point to one single word in the Constitution and the Bill of Rights where abortion is expressed or expressly implied. The abortionists went to the Supreme Court to press their case, when it should have been taken up by the Congress. Abortion, in any case, would be a matter for the States under the 10th Amendment, called "police powers" of the states to regulate health, welfare and police protection of the people of the states. The 10th Amendment was written to keep the Federal Government from interfering in such matters.

Appendix, Congressional Record, June 30, 1890, page 696:

Were Mr. Jefferson here today, he would tell this House that judges appointed to office on account of their political views and holding the office from and looking to preferment at the hands of the party in power will in many cases be influenced by political bias...

I am sensible of the inroads daily taking the Federal Government into the jurisdiction of its coordinates, the States governments...

The judiciary branch is the instrument, which working like gravity, without intermission, is to press us at last into one consolidated mass...

If Congress fails to shield the States from dangers so palpable and so imminent, then the States must shield themselves and meet the invader. Foot to foot...

In March 4, 1823, Mr. Jefferson wrote to Judge Johnson and in closing the letter he said: I can not lay down my pen without referring to one of the subjects of my former letter, for the truth is there is no danger I apprehend so much as the consolidation of our government by the noiseless and therefore un-alarming instrumentality of the Supreme Court.

And with no body of men is this restraint more warranted than with the judges of what is commonly called the General Government, but what I call our foreign department.

They are practicing upon the Constitution by inference, analogies and sophism, as they would on ordinary law.

But it has been proved that the power of declaring the law ad libitum, by sapping and mining slowly and without alarm the foundations of the Constitution can do what open forums would not dare to attempt. I have not observed whether in your code you have provided against causing judicial decisions and for judges to give their opinions seriatim, every man for him.

In the foregoing is found all of the tenets that went into the Supreme Court ruling on Roe vs. Wade, and with it, the much wider implication that not only did the court purport to allow infants to be aborted, but the Supreme Court on that day, aborted also the Constitution and the Bill of Rights. One of the worst disasters ever to befall the United States was the passing by the Supreme Court of Roe vs. Wade, which purportedly makes abortions legal, it behooves us to take stock of just where we are at, and what road we as a nation will travel in the next fifty years.

The following is a chronology of how the crime of child murder became "legal."

1973 - Roe vs. Wade

Norma McCorvey, alias "Doe," was used by the radical feminist inheritors of the Communist Hull House "feminists" of the Roosevelt era to claim as her constitutional "right," a "right" to abortion on demand. Instead of refusing to hear the case on the grounds that Congress and not the Supreme Court make the laws, the Court ruled 7-2 that abortion was a right and not a crime.

Justice Harry Blackmun wrote the following words that sent the grim reaper riding across the land to reap a harvest of millions of tiny mangled corpses; the most defenseless of the defenseless slaughtered with no one to help them:

The right to privacy (the 4th Amendment) is broad enough to encompass a women's decision whether or not to terminate her pregnancy.

Blackmun had not one shred of constitutional evidence to support his preposterous position, and in my opinion, at that moment the man took leave of his senses, or else his simplistic interpretation was taken directly from the Communist Manifesto of 1848. What Blackmun did, and for which he should have been removed from the bench, was to stretch and squeeze the Constitution to fit his own predilections that is forbidden by the 9th Amendment which is aimed against judges doing just that.

On that day not only were infant babies denied the right to life, liberty and property under the Constitution (for children follow the condition of the parents), but the Constitution was mangled the way their tiny corpses were soon to be mangled. Henceforth, not only discarded, aborted babies would be consigned to the dumpsters in back alleys, but also, the Constitution.

Roe vs. Wade was not a matter for the jurisdiction of the Court, but solely a matter for the Congress, since the courts have no constitutional power to legislate. Only Congress could have passed a constitutional amendment, which would have first gone to the States for ratification. Only then would abortion have become law. But a cowardly Congress ducked the issue and allowed the Supreme Court to usurp the function of the law-makers, thereby permitting the court to find a power in the Constitution which did not exist and has never existed.

It reminded me so much of the time when President Woodrow Wilson was working to send thousands of young

American soldiers to their death on the European battlefields in WWI, but admitted that he had no authority to conscript the militia for military service abroad. Congress recognizing that it had no authority to send the militia to Europe, thereupon "gave permission" for Wilson to do so in flagrant violation of the Constitution. (For further reading please see my book, What You Should Know About the U.S. Constitution.)

The mental contortionists of the Supreme Court somehow stretched the 4th Amendment to include a women's "right" to have an abortion, just as Wilson stretched his non-existent presidential powers to order the conscripted militia to fight in Europe.

The Supreme Court in so doing violated the 9th Amendment which expressly forbids judges from writing their predilections into law. The court was guilty of violating the 5th, 9th and 10th Amendments with its ruling Roe vs. Wade, and Congress should have assembled at once to overturn this grave assault on the Constitution, which it has the power to do.

The 1973 Roe vs. Wade ruling spawned a whole new industry; bloody charnel houses complete with a lexicon of newspeak language such as: "health providers," "trimester," "family planning," "clinics," "pro-choice," "reproductive rights," "planned parenthood," "reproductive health services," "clinic escorts," "contraception," "reproductive decisions," "reproductive freedom," ad infinitum.

1973 - Doe vs. Bolton

In a 7-2 decision, the Supreme Court struck down a Georgia State law that a doctor must concur with a woman's decision to have an abortion during the first "trimester" (three months) of pregnancy.

This was yet a further violation of the 10th Amendment, which declares emphatically that such matters reside with the States and that the Central Government cannot interfere in health and family matters which are outside of the jurisdiction of the central government. By its Doe vs. Bolton ruling, the Supreme Court was indicating that it would brook no attacks on its Roe vs. Wade ruling, an attitude to which it has remained staunchly wedded, ever since. What is meant by "police powers" shorthand, so often used to describe the provisions of the 10th Amendment?

> "Police powers consist of health, welfare, education, family matters, State laws and police protection. They are always collectively referred to as 'police powers of the States'."

Clearly, these rights are States rights and cannot be infringed upon or interfered with by the Central Government as the States never relinquished their rights over such matters when they joined the Union. Pomeroy, the great constitutionalist, says in his work, Constitutional Law:

> ... those affairs which are local affect the citizen in his private capacity under the Constitution has to do with private and personal rights and not the Federal Government abstracted from his relations to the whole political society, are managed by the separate State Governments which were found in existence and left remaining by the same Constitution.

In addition we have:

9 Wallace 41:

> No power is conferred by the Constitution upon the Congress to establish mere police regulations within the States.

14 Howard 17:

> The power to make municipal regulations (State laws) for the restraint and punishment of crime, for the preservation of health and the morals of her citizens has never been surrendered by the States or restrained by the Constitution of the United States.

1976 - Planned Parenthood of Central Missouri vs. Danforth

In a 5-4 ruling, the court struck down a state law which said that the father or parents of an unborn child had the right to prevent abortion taking place. This outright assault on "equal under the law" gave special rights to women, and denied them to men and the unborn infant — one of the most heinous but seldom commented upon outcomes of the Roe vs. Wade ruling. Here again, the court legislated as there is no provision in the Constitution and the Bill of Rights that would allow discrimination; giving special rights to the mother of the child and denying the father the right to protect the life of his child and denying the child its right to protection under the 5th Amendment.

In this case, the 5th Amendment was once again violently assaulted.

1979 - Bellotti vs. Bairdl

In a unanimous decision, the court struck down a Massachusetts law which allowed parents of minors to prevent them from having abortions. As can be seen by the foregoing cases as well as those which were to follow, the Supreme Court was carrying out, almost to the letter, the policy of "free love" (sexual relations 17 without responsibilities) introduced by the Soviet Commissar Madame Kollontei in her tour during the U.S. in the 1920s. The one thing which stands out like a lighthouse on a dark night is that abortion, also known as "free love," is a doctrine of the Communists. Here again in this ruling, the 10th Amendment was ripped to shreds by the Supreme Court.

1979 - Colautti vs. Franklin

In this case the court struck down a Pennsylvania law by a margin of 6-3 that a doctor is duty-bound to save the life of an aborted baby, if the doctor believed that the life of the child could be saved. Am I dreaming, or is this nightmare really taking place in the United States? May God forgive us! Here is a most diabolical "law" which says: "Doctor, don't you dare go to the aid of that baby struggling and writhing, gasping for air, its tiny fists clenched in agony, clinging to life, having somehow, miraculously, survived your every attempt to kill it!" What kind of a person would walk by a wounded dog without attempting to render assistance? People are marshaled by the hundreds and rush to the beach in an attempt to save a stranded whale, a stranded dolphin. The fire brigade gets called out to rescue a cat stranded in a treetop. But to help a struggling new-born child clinging to life, "Doctor, don't you dare do such a thing!" It is no wonder the Muslim nations call America "The Great Satan."

1993 - Akron vs. Akron Center For Reproductive Health

In a 6-3 ruling the court struck down an Akron, Ohio, city ordinance requiring all abortions after the "trimester" period to be performed in hospitals after a 24-hour waiting period, and also struck down the provision in the same ordinance, which required doctors to inform the women contemplating abortion of the serious side-effects, both medical and emotional and that the "fetus" (euphemism for a baby) is a living human being, from the moment of conception. Why don't women who have abortions go to regular hospitals for this most serious medical procedure?

The reason is that they want their child to be murdered in private and they do not want hospital records, which can under certain circumstances be made public, testifying to what they have done.

This is why thousands of charnel-house human butcher shops have sprung up like poison mushrooms all over the country. When a woman allows her infant child to be murdered, she wants the foul deed done in privacy!

1986

The court reaffirmed its Roe vs. Wade ruling and by a vote of 5-4 struck down a Pennsylvania "informed consent" law mandating that women seeking abortion first be given counseling about the state of their unborn baby and their right to child support from the father, as well as the risks attached to abortion. Here again, the court grossly violated the 5th, 9th and 10th Amendments.

1992 - Planned Parenthood of Southeastern Pennsylvania vs. Casey

In a 5-4 vote the court upheld Roe vs. Wade, but did not refer to the alleged right as "fundamental" and struck down a State law which said that the husband or father of the child was to be notified before the women went ahead with the execution of her child. Here again, the 5th Amendment right of the father and the infant were flagrantly violated by the Supreme Court as was the 10th Amendment.

1993 - Bray vs. Alexandria Women's Health Clinic

In a 5-4 vote the court ruled that a law which came into effect after the Civil War to control Klan activities could be invoked against demonstrators protesting outside of an abortion "clinic."

The Congress later violated the Constitution by passing a "law" which held that freedom of access to "clinics" could not be blocked, the so-called "Freedom of Access to Clinics Act." Here again, the 10th Amendment was grossly violated.

1994 - NOW vs. Scheidler

On January 24, 1994, the Supreme Court ruled in favor of a case brought by the National Organization of Women (NOW) on behalf of two abortion charnel houses in Delaware and Ohio under the so-called "RICO" statute, in itself one hundred percent unconstitutional. By unanimous consent the court held that RICO - the so-called Federal

Government anti-racketeering law -could be invoked against demonstrators gathered outside a charnel-house "clinic" to protest the murder of infant children, going on inside.

This ruling is the worst anti-family pro-abortion ruling ever handed down by the court and should have long ago been overturned by the Congress. The mangled First Amendment rights of the protesters against child murder were thrown into the "clinic's" alley-dumpster along with the mangled remains of murdered children.

This was by far the most flagrant violation of the U.S. Constitution and the Bill of Rights since Roe vs. Wade and typified more than anything else what Jefferson wrote to Judge Johnson, which I quoted earlier herein from Appendix, Congressional Record, June 30, 1890. It echoes the warning given by Jefferson that justices of the Supreme Court would be the instrument for overriding State's rights. It was another case of the court legislating, instead of the Congress, and Congress has thus far failed to do its duty by overturning this "law."

The Supreme Court ruling in this case nullified the right of citizens to gather for a peaceful demonstration and it stifled the right of free speech by saying that anyone who protested outside of the charnel houses would be considered as engaging in "racketeering." The court took no cognizance that its ruling grossly violated the 10th Amendment and in an attempt to justify the convoluted reasoning, Justice Rehnquist wrote:

> Acts such as the alleged extortion may not benefit the protesters financially but may still drain money from the economy by harming businesses such as clinics.

3

INFANT MURDER IS A BUSINESS

There you have it; henceforth places of infant murder were to be classed as "businesses" and peaceful demonstrators would be classed as racketeers extorting money from abortion houses. The great St. George Tucker would have slapped Rehnquist down very quickly were he alive today. Here is what St. George Tucker had to say on the subject of attempts by the Federal Government to abridge the right of assembly:

> The Congress of the United States possesses no power to regulate, or interfere with the domestic concerns of any State, it belongs to them (the States) to establish any rules respecting the rights of property, nor will the Constitution permit any prohibition of arms to the people, or peaceful assemblies by them for whatever purpose, and in any number, whatsoever they see fit...

(Blackstone's Commentaries on the U.S. Constitution, page 315.) We should not care what Mr. Justice Rehnquist had to say on the matter; St. George Tucker was a great master of the Constitution which Rehnquist could never be. NOW vs. Scheidler is one hundred percent unconstitutional and must be overturned at the very first opportunity. Were John Marshall, our first Chief Justice of the Supreme Court alive, here is what he would have told Rehnquist:

Congress is empowered to make exceptions to the appellate jurisdiction as to the law and fact of the Supreme Court. These exceptions certainly go as far as the legislature may think for the interest and the liberty of the people.

What Marshall said was the legislature has the right to overturn any act of the Supreme Court where it deems such acts to be against "the interests and the liberty of the people." As NOW vs. Scheidler qualifies for overturning, as does abortion, then we must ask ourselves, "why hasn't Congress taken the appropriate action?" With the Supreme Court ruling, the United States entered into the most dangerous period of its history where gross violations of the Constitution and the Bill of Rights would go unchallenged. If a group of unelected judges can make such sweeping rules and the Central Government can apply them without reaction from the Congress — supposedly representing the people — then indeed liberty has perished in this country and the Constitution has become labia raza, a scribbling pad.

The liberals did their best to try and make out that the RICO ruling did not have blanket coverage implications, but the truth is that as the "law" now stands, it can applied to ANY group of protesters on the most specious grounds that it would "drain money from the economy."

Madsen vs. Women's Health Center

In a vote of 6-3 the court upheld a lower court ruling establishing "buffer zones" around abortion charnel houses so as to ensure a woman her right to enter the "clinic" and exercise her "reproductive rights" to have her child murdered.

At the same time the court said the "buffer zone" had to be set up in such a way that it would not interfere with the 1st Amendment rights of the protesters. The tragedy of abortion, apart from the millions of lives lost, is that few seem to understand that abortion is a matter upon which the Congress should have legislated by way of a constitutional amendment.

Abortion falls under the 10th Amendment and it is a matter over which the Central Government has no jurisdiction. Thus it is in the States where the battle against this evil of abortion will be 22 won or lost, and that is why it is so important for the States to send delegates to Congress who will no longer tolerate the central government violating the 10th Amendment. The hope is that the Republican Party will wake up to this truth.

The Republican Party does not need "liberals" or "moderates" such as Congressmen Hyde, Firestone, Bob Dole or Pres. H. W. Bush and Nicholson, the Republican Party Chairman, in its ranks.

It wants and needs stalwarts who are firmly committed to the great battle of overturning Roe vs. Wade.

All it will take is for a simple majority in the Congress to vote to overturn Roe vs. Wade. Congress has the right to take such action, as the Supreme Court is not coequal with the Congress, and neither is the Executive branch. To help those who may not be clear about the constitutional issues involved, abortion has no Constitutional mandate, and is therefore, ultra-vires, making it crystal clear that Roe vs. Wade is a constitutional nullity, of no effect, and no law at all, and incumbent upon none to obey.

The United States Supreme Court was tricked by the extreme left women's organizations, more particularly, the National Organization of Women (NOW) and the National Abortion Rights League (NARL), in Roe vs. Wade and Doe vs. Bolton.

The problem is that in establishing the error of the decision to make abortion legal one has to search through masses of pages of the Congressional Record, where this information lies buried under anonymous titles not found in the Congressional Record index. Judges of the Supreme Court ought to have done their research into this mass of documentation which proves that abortion is unconstitutional, but they obviously failed to do so.

Some appointed judges may not even know of its existence.

Some of the information proving abortion has no place in the U.S. Constitution is found in the Congressional Record of the 1920s, juxta-positioned alongside the debates that exposed the 23

Fabian-Socialist drive to move in on American politics. But for the watchfulness of a Congress of the period, which differs so vastly from today's Congress, the bid by the Communists, Socialists and Fabianists to take over the United States of America in the 1920s was turned back. But these evil forces never gave up the struggle, of which abortion rights is a very important part, having been taken straight out of the Communist Manifesto of 1848. The following are where some of the proofs that abortion is not a "right" nor can it be legal are found in the Congressional Record, although this is by no means a complete list:

Congressional Record, House

Pages: 4582-4590 Senate7018-7064 April 24, 1924 592-618 January 7, 1924 4154-4170 February 1924 12918-12951 July 2, 1926

The Senate debates on Roe vs. Wade are contained in the following:

Congressional Record, Senate

Pages: SI 1525-11570 September 1924 11501-11523, 11547-11570.

The first fact we must note is that the U.S. Supreme Court in at least two decisions ruled that the U.S. Constitution and the Bill of Rights are Christian documents. The last decision handed down by the Court to this effect was in 1900. Research has shown that there is not a vestige of truth in the notion that the Constitution and the Bill of Rights supports or in any way grants the right of abortion. In order to fully understand the U.S. Constitution and its provisions, we first have to take note of the delegated powers of Congress, called the primary powers of Congress, and look for 24 that power, or Article 1, Section 8, Clauses 1-18.

The power of abortion as a legal right has to be expressly implied in the Constitution or it has to be incidental to another power in the Constitution. Such expressly implied law is known as statutory law.

Under its auxiliary power, Congress has one opportunity to go further than just an expressly implied power; it has the power in Clause 18 to imply power:

> To make all laws which shall be necessary and proper for
> carrying into execution the foregoing powers, and all other
> powers vested in the U.S. Constitution and government of
> the United States, or in any department or officer thereof
> The two words that give the Congress and Senate implied
> powers are the words "necessary" and "proper."

Nowhere in the U.S. Constitution and the Bill of Rights is
there an expressed or implied grant-in-power for abortion.

The other powers mentioned are called the secondary
powers of Congress, and it is the Legislative Branch that
makes laws. The courts cannot make laws save and except
on a case by case basis, and then, Congress and the Senate,
still have to approve any judicial decision and enact it into
law through the legislative department.

The modern notion, nurtured by "Eastern Liberal
Establishment" law professors is that somehow the
Supreme Court is coequal with the Congress, which is 100
percent wrong.

In fact the Congress has the power to suspend the Supreme
Court, and indeed it once did so during the McCardle case.
I shudder when I hear the pro-aborticide adherents of the
Communist Manifesto of 1848 say:

> "Oh well, the Supreme Court will eventually decide the
> issue."

The Supreme Court cannot legislate even though it is
constantly striving to do so. Therefore it does not have the
last word on legislation or the Constitution. All judges have
to adhere to the U.S. Constitution, including justices of the
Supreme Court.

Article VI, Part 1, U.S. Constitution:

> The Constitution, and the laws of the United States shall be made in pursuance thereof; (the word "pursuance"-does not actually mean the direct words of the Constitution) and all treaties made, or shall be made, under the authority of the United States, shall be the supreme law of the land; and the Judges in every State shall be bound thereby, anything in the Constitution or laws of any State to the contrary notwithstanding.

This applies with equal force to town and city councils that pass ordinances which are at variance with the Constitution, such as happened in Redwood City and San Jose, California in 1986. The actions of these councils, who were trying to protect abortion charnel houses against public protest demonstrations, are 100 percent illegal. Police officers who uphold such illegal ordinances are in violation of the rights of citizens to protest under the U.S. Constitution.

The Supreme Court was never meant to be sequestered from the sovereign people; originally the judges journeyed from State to State on horseback. Supreme Court judges are the servants of we, the sovereign people as much as are any other public servants. They cannot go outside of the Constitution.

The aura of majesty and power that surrounds the Supreme Court is a false aura. We must not be intimidated by it.

If the right to abortion is not found in the Constitution and the Bill of Rights, from whence then springs this evil practice?

The plain truth is that "abortion rights" come directly from the Communist Manifesto of 1848.

The U.S. Constitution and the Bill of Rights are not compatible with the Communist Manifesto of 1848; the U.S. Constitution cannot be compromised by any judicial decision, such as taken by local officials through local ordinances (of which "gun control" measures are a good example). This applies to all judicial decisions and to the Legislative Branch of government, local, state and federal. There is no compromise possible with the U.S.

Constitution and the Communist Manifesto of 1848, yet this is precisely what happened in the free love abortion case called Roe vs. Wade, in which the person bringing the case, did not have the decency or the courage to use her own name, but resorted to an alias.

In the 19th century, abortion was better known as infanticide. Now the American people are supposed to pay for "free love," better described as irresponsible actions, by funding abortions directly and indirectly. The following must be noted with great care: The U.S. Supreme Court decision on Roe vs. Wade was taken straight out of the pages of Communism and Family, authored by Alexandra Kollontei, an early champion of women's rights and the right to an abortion. Confirmation of my statement is found in the Congressional Record, pages 12944 of pages 12851-12918, July 3, 1926, "Maternity and Infancy Act."

The Endowment of Motherhood is another attack on the family, and only slightly less communistic than Communism and the Family, authored by Engels, the Leninist-Socialist. Bebel, the hero of the French

Revolution, was yet another rabid hardcore Communist whose work, Women and Socialism, provided most of the spurious unconstitutional arguments used in the court cases that gave us the evil of Roe vs. Wade, and in addition, many of Bebel's ideas are found in the lexicon of the propaganda of the National Organization of Women (NOW) and the National Abortion Rights League (NARL).

4

WHO WAS MADAME KOLLONTEI?

W ho was Madame Alexandra Kollontei, the real author of "abortion rights" and the unseen, carefully-hidden inspirer of NARL and NOW and their Marxist-Leninist-Socialist "feminists?"

> Madame Kollontei is now Soviet minister to Norway, after a hectic career which included eight husbands, two positions as people's commissar-first commissar of welfare, two visits to the United States (in 1915 and 1916) as a German Socialist agitator, after having been deported from three European countries, in 1914, a dangerous revolutionist...

> Page 9972 in 9962-9977 Senate, Congressional Record, and May 31, 1924.

Then, a further expose of this champion of "abortion rights" was given by Representative Sosnowsky:

> ... Recently there came to Mexico as the ambassador of the Soviet Union one Alexandra Kollontei. She is said to be a clever leader in the world revolutionary movement for 28 years; that she has been arrested in three different countries because of her efforts of 1916 and in 1917 she visited the United States speaking from coast to coast.

> She was under the management of Ludwig Lore, now a prominent Communist in the United States. The object and

purpose of the visit of Kollontei to the United States in 1916 and 1917, was to incite the socialists of this country and to hamper our activities if the United States entered through a system of nonresistance by what took place. Alexandra Kollontei is the world's greatest exponent of 'free love' and nationalization of children. She is in Mexico for that purpose and bodes no good to the people of the United States...

Page 4599 of pages 4582-4604, House, Congressional Record, February 23, 1927.

These words were to prove almost prophetic. In them are found the origin of the feminist movement in the U.S. and it is clear that its leaders, Bella Abzug, Kate Michelmas and Eleanor Smeal, worked in the shadow of Alexandra Kollontei.

Kollontei's book, *Communism and the Family*, is the most violent and savage attack on marriage and the family ever written, surpassing the decadent evil of Frederic Engels' *The Origin of the Family*.

Her free love radical followers formerly called themselves the International League of Peace and Freedom, but have since undergone a lot of name changes to disguise the fact that their agenda is the same as that of Alexandra Kollontei, and today they call themselves the National Organization of Women (NOW) and the National Abortion Rights League (NARL).

The goals of these "liberal feminists" who, if they were honest, would call themselves Socialists, are the same as the Socialist-Communists of the 1920s. Here is exposed the origin of the clamor of NOW and NARL for abortion rights (free love without responsibility). They, and their incendiary liberal allies in the House and Senate in an unholy alliance with the kept controlled jackals of the news media, were able to dupe the Supreme Court in making its decision in Roe vs. Wade. NOW would have delighted P.T. Barnum, the great circus showman, who said "the American people love to be humbugged." Joseph Stalin put it even more bluntly, after his triumph at Yalta:

> ... They are gullible and easily deceived by illusions which their media are past-masters at creating. We have only to change a few names here, a few names there and they believe that these organizations no longer exist, and they will believe it... We must make the most of the gullible beliefs of the American people and their leaders. We must drop the existing Communist labels and replace them with Socialist ones...

Evidently, for the Marxist-Leninist feminists under Kollontei who ran the "International League of Peace and Freedom," Stalin's advice had merit; they became NOW and NARL under the umbrella of women's rights. NOW and NARL are doing a good job in humbugging so many young women whom they are grossly misleading, and who are in total ignorance of the fact that abortion is not mentioned in the Constitution or the Bill of Rights, nor in the rights reserved for we, the sovereign people. In this, NOW and NARL are greatly helped by the media who are past masters at deceiving the American people by illusions, as Stalin so accurately observed.

No part of the U.S. Constitution can be isolated from any other part. Every part of the U.S. Constitution has to be read and interpreted in the light of the whole Constitution.

It cannot be fragmented. To call a child in the womb a non-person is about as twisted as we could get in Roe vs. Wade and Doe vs. Bolton. Radical "feminist" movements are not a new thing. The Marxist-Leninist-Fabian Socialists nearly overcame the U.S. in 1924, and they used radical feminists to this end throughout the 1920s. There is nothing in the 14th Amendment that would grant abortion rights. As Judge Story said, most judges, and especially those appointed by Pres. Franklin D. Roosevelt to pack the Supreme Court, failed in constitutional interpretation; instead, they have read their own thoughts into it, which is predilection. As Senator Sam Ervin said, they found something new in the Constitution and the Bill of Rights.

The cunning deceptions of the 13th, 14th and 15th Amendments did not fool all judges. The Slaughterhouse judges poked fun at the three dishonest amendments. It may or may not be known, but in the Negro vote, the Republican Party saw an opportunity to remain in power, so it cobbled the three amendments together in haste. But the amendments did not include the "right" to have an abortion.

The first intent of the 14th Amendment was to ensure that Confederate officers who served at State level and those with the rank of Colonel or higher were debarred from serving as public officers. So anxious were the Republicans to rush the 14th Amendment through, that they forgot to give the Negro the right to hold public office - this only came with the 15th Amendment.

Far too much has been read into the 14th Amendment that is not in it at all. Those who have seriously studied the Reconstruction debates know that the 14th Amendment (and the 15th) must be taken with a large grain of salt. They are essentially, not part of the U.S. Constitution.

In a display of twisting and squeezing the Constitution to fit the agenda of Liberals, Socialists and their supporters in Congress, the Warren Court used the 14th Amendment to mean anything they wanted it to mean; which added up to rampant predilection.

There is not one grain of evidence to support the Roe vs. Wade decision by the Supreme Court.

The 14th Amendment does not state abortion, nor is it expressly implied, therefore abortion as a power cannot be taken.

The entire U.S. Constitution can be seen in the 5th Amendment, protection of life, liberty and property, and it is expressly implied that life in the womb is protected.

A simple way to test the legislation that made Roe vs. Wade law is to see if it is found in the delegated powers of Congress or 31 incidental to another delegated power. On this count alone, the proposed legislation to make Roe vs. Wade something other than case law, completely fails.

What the Supreme Court attempted to do in Roe vs. Wade was fill in between amendments, which it cannot do. The 9th Amendment was written expressly to prevent judges from filling in amendments not in the Constitution.

The U.S. Supreme Court went outside the U.S. Constitution in Roe vs. Wade and Doe vs. Bolton; these were case law decisions and not constitutional law. The U.S. Constitution cannot be made over by case law, but only by amendments ratified by all 50 States.

NOW and NARL knew that they could never get all 50 States to ratify an amendment to the Constitution to make abortion legal, so they and their incendiary liberal supporters in the House and Senate, aided by illusions created by the media, fought to get abortion legalized via the back door — in this case, the Supreme Court.

Roe vs. Wade is a prescription for anarchy. Anarchy is defined as "the abolition of formal government and free action for the individual... "

The cry of the abortionists "freedom of choice" has naught to do with the Constitution, but is an anarchist's cry. Where in the Constitution is the right to draw the taxpayers into mass murder of babies and force them to pay for these vile murders? It is not there! Roe vs. Wade and Doe vs. Bolton have no force and effect in law in the States as the 5th Amendment fully protects both the born and the unborn child in the mother's womb. Abortion is not allowed by the U.S. Constitution, and certainly not in the 4th Amendment in spite of what Justice Rehnquist said. Another way the Communist collectives twist and squeeze the Constitution is found in the teaching by liberal law professors who try to include 32 the Preamble to the Constitution in the body of the Constitution.

In fact, the Preamble to the Constitution has nothing to do with the U.S. Constitution and the Bill of Rights.

To make the Preamble a part of the Constitution would "turn it into a blank paper" to use the words of Thomas Jefferson. The Marxist-Communist Liberals in the House and Senate have, over a 50-year period, sought to overturn limits placed, for example, on welfare, and turn this nation into a Socialist welfare paradise - and now they want poor women to have abortions while on welfare!

These incendiaries and their "Eastern Liberal Establishment" law professors have successfully isolated Article I, Section 8, Clause I from the balance of Section 8. The limits on the welfare clause are found in other parts of Section 8, Article I. It is the auxiliary clause, or article I, Section 8, Clause 18, with the words "necessary" and "proper," that defines how far the general welfare should go.

That these liberal Senators do not know the Constitution is shown by the fact that 90 percent of them do not know what constitutes a declaration of war, nor have they the faintest idea of how to write one. That is why President G.W. Bush got away with his illegal war against Iraq. Had the Senate done its constitutional duty, Bush would have been stopped in his tracks, impeached and tried for treason, and removed from office if found guilty. What the Senate did was to interpret the Constitution by giving Bush "permission" to attack Iraq, which was not a declaration of war. The House and Senate hashed up an utterly feeble substitute for a declaration of war, entirely unconstitutional and without a shred of legality.

Exactly the same thing can be said about the so-called Supreme Court decision to allow abortion. The Supreme Court had no right to pass such a law any more than George W. Bush had the right to order U.S. armed forces to invade Iraq.

We had the same type of total disregard for the Constitution in the Au Coin bill, which called for taxpayer's money to be used to fund abortions for women in the armed services. The bill enlarged the gross error made by the Supreme Court in Roe vs. Wade. Au Coin's "free love" bill is unconstitutional. Nowhere is abortion expressed in the Constitution nor is it incidental to any other part of the Constitution.

Page S10078, Congressional Record, Senate, July 18, 1991 tells more on the terrible saga of the Senate trying to push changes on Title X.

> ... That purpose is clear; the purpose of Title X is not to perform abortions, not to refer for abortion, or to tout abortion. Pregnant women do not need preventative services offered by Title X...

These comments were made by Senator Orrin Hatch. Here again we have a further chapter in the tragedy of mass child murder being played out in the Senate, where certain Socialist members try to put a legal face on the crime of ripping a defenseless baby from the mother's womb; unconstitutional murder that flies in the face of common sense. Common sense is the essence of the U.S. Constitution, and yet the Marxist-Communist Liberals continue to defy the tradition of common sense.

The Supreme Court acted in a most ridiculous and absurd manner, without any common sense, in purporting to make abortion legal.

Common sense law is centuries old, and dates back hundreds of years to the War of the Roses in England. The number of babies murdered each year (approximately 1.8 million) as a result of the tragic absurdity called Roe vs. Wade is greater than the number of soldiers of both armies who died during the Civil War. How can abortion be classed as common sense law springing from Natural Law? John Adams and Thomas Jefferson must be whirling in their graves at the very thought of such an odious perversion.

5

JUDGE STORY DECLARES ABORTION NON COMMON SENSE

Judge Joseph Story covers this aspect brilliantly in his ten rules of interpretation of the U.S. Constitution in his third volume on the U.S. Constitution, pages 398-441. Senator Robert Dole, who once tried to become the president of the United States, also does not know the Constitution as he ought to. His "National Registration Act for Federal Elections," page S10428, Congressional Record, Senate, July 18, 1991, is 100 percent wrong, as the bill violates Article I, Section 4, Part I of the Constitution. In any case, Senator Dole ought to know that there is no such thing as "Federal Elections." Senators are elected by the states not the Federal Government, which has no voters.

At least Dole's bill gives an indication in the title of what the bill is about; most bills to do with abortion are hidden by deceptive titles that give no inkling of abortion in the title. A good example is "National Institute of Health Revitalization Amendment of 1991, H.R. 2507," which is an abortion bill. (Pages 5826-5879, Congressional Record, Senate.)

There are still a few good men in the House and Senate, although their numbers dwindle with each election. One such man was Representative Smith of Rhode Island who said:

Madame Chairman, the issue of informed consent is an issue here as well. Who gives it, according to the Waxman bill? The mother, who has abandoned the child to the abortionist's knife.

Unlike a baby who dies in a miscarriage where the parent stands foursquare in promoting the child's welfare and well-being, a parent who abandons a child to the abortionist, has demonstrated no such concern...

(Page H5833, Congressional Record, House, July 23rd 1991).

Being discussed was a chamber of horrors bill that would allow bogus "scientific experiments" using tissues of the babies who fell victim to burning saline or the knife of the abortionist.

Congressman Henry Waxman's bill was nothing but a series of Marxist-Communist-Socialist proposals that would have drawn applause from Kollontei, Engels, Marx, Eleanor Roosevelt and Miss Jane Adams, the former Socialist leader of Hull House, the creator of women Socialists.

Waxman's bill, and the very evil thing that gave it life, Roe vs. Wade, is as worthless, constitutionally speaking, as the so-called United Nations Treaty (?) Agreement (?) passed in 1945 in violation of the U.S. Constitution. Yet thousands of our soldiers have died in wars because of its provisions and many thousands more will die in coming wars.

Millions of babies have died, and millions more will die under the lawless, asinine, ridiculous Roe vs. Wade Supreme Court ruling.

Roe vs. Wade is an abomination beyond the pale of the U.S. Constitution, and as such, have no standing in terms of U.S. law.

On page 12942 of the Congressional Record of July 3, 1926, the aims and objectives of the Marxist-Communist-Socialist believers are spelled out:

> Three Objects of the Communist Manifesto. The three main purposes of the Communist Manifesto of 1848 by Marx and Engels are, destruction of the monogamous family, destruction of private property and the destruction of countries and nationalities.

> The manifesto declares "abolition of the family" etc. It is clear that abortion is a Communist tool to break up the monogamous family and to break down nation-states.

On page 12942 of the above Congressional Record, we find the following:

> The Overman Committee on Bolshevism of the United States Senate.

> The apparent purpose of the Bolshevik government (of Russia) is to make the Russian citizen, especially the women and children, wards dependent on that government... It has destroyed the natural ambition and made impossible of accomplishment the moral obligation to provide care for, and adequately protect the child of his blood and the mother of that child against the misfortunes orphan hood and widowhood...

> They have promulgated decrees relating to marriage and divorce which practically establish "free love."

So what the Supreme Court did in Roe vs. Wade was to borrow from the writings of an avowed anti-family Communist, Madame Kollontei, other Bolshevik writers and the Bolshevik legal system and give it form, thereby placing free love irresponsibility above the level of the monogamous family. The Supreme Court was attempting to reconcile the Communist Manifesto of 1848 with the U.S. Constitution. Probably under political duress in the Roe vs. Wade case, the Supreme Court failed to properly read the 5th Amendment, which not only protects present life, but also "pre-life."

What the Supreme Court did was to twist and squeeze the U.S. Constitution, which grants no Natural Law authority to state that a "fetus" in the third month of development is not a person. There is absolutely no Constitutional basis for this false statement nor 37 does the word "fetus" appear anywhere in the Constitution and the Bill of Rights.

What the Supreme Court did in Roe vs. Wade was twist and squeeze the U.S. Constitution to fit the Communist Manifesto of 1848, and they did this when they declared abortion a legal right, because nowhere in the Constitution and the Bill of Rights is it stated that abortion is a right.

When the U.S. Constitution is silent on a power and is not incidental to another power, in the words of the first Chief Justice of the United States, Justice John Marshall, it is an inhibition (prohibition) of that power. This is a corollary to the 9th Amendment to the U.S. Constitution which was meant to apply chiefly to judges.

Whenever the judiciary, legislative and executive departments go outside the boundaries of the U.S.

Constitution, their actions have no force in law. A clear example of going outside of the U.S. Constitution to enforce statutes and ordinances is that of the City Council of San Jose California, whose Mayor Susan Hammer knows absolutely nothing about the restrictions placed by the Constitution on those who would seek to misuse the Constitution to support their cause. Mayor Hammer sought to deny anti-abortionists the use of public sidewalks outside of charnel houses (abortion mills) to protest murders taking place. The ordinance passed by Hammer and her fellow council members to deny demonstrators the use of public sidewalks outside of abortion charnel houses, must be struck down. Such ordinances are an attack upon the Constitution. I examined the San Jose anti-abortion protest ordinance and found it to be an almost carbon copy of a bill proposed by California Senator Boxer, a devout follower of the teachings of Kollontei.

The U.S. Supreme Court Judges tried to alter the Constitution by their own thinking which is predilection, a process that has gathered momentum since Roe vs. Wade, so that what we have 38 today are not Constitutional amendments passed by all 50 states, but 0 amendments dreamed up and executed by judicial fiat - absolutely without any force and effect in terms of the Constitution and the Bill of Rights. The predilections of the Supreme Court in gun control measures and abortion rights adopted by lower courts, city and state governments is a dangerous situation which must be halted. The big lie here is that somehow, the privacy right of the Fourth Amendment, and abortion rights are compatible or as some NOW people would have it, "the same thing."

THERE IS NO RELATIONSHIP BETWEEN THE
FOURTH AMENDMENT AND ABORTION.

Abortion is a moral tenet, and in the U.S., until the Marxist-Communist Socialists took over, abortion was a crime, and under Natural Law it remains so.

The 9th Amendment of the U.S. Constitution makes null and void any relationship between abortion and privacy. The far-left NOW, does not want its members to hear that "abortion rights" come straight out of Communist doctrines and not out of the U.S. Constitution and the Bill of Rights, Natural Law or the Christian religion.

The 9th Amendment is a restriction on federal government:

> The enumeration in the Constitution of certain rights shall not be construed to deny or disparage others (or other rights not enumerated) retained by the people.

It follows that because certain rights are not enumerated in the Constitution and Bill of Rights, the Federal Government cannot override subvert or usurp rights not directly enumerated.

Government cannot attempt to fill in their predilections between the lines of the Constitution. An amendment to the Constitution 39 can only become law if the amendment is passed by all the States.

The 9th Amendment, does not grant government, the Supreme Court, the National Organization of Women, Comrade Boxer and the members of the City Council of San Jose or any other body, the right to twist and squeeze a construction out of that which is not in the U.S. Constitution and the Bill of Rights, or those rights already in the Constitution and Bill of Rights.

To put a finer point on it, the first 10 amendments to the U.S. Constitution are a restriction on the Federal Government. There are some who say that the 5th Amendment is shared with the Federal Government. To properly understand the 9th Amendment, we need to research the Annals of Congress in the debates on the 9th Amendment, which we find in the History of Congress, Annals of Congress, pages 421-780, which deals with the proposed 9th Amendment, June 1789:

> Mr. Madison... It has been objected also against a bill of rights, that by enumerating particular exceptions to the grant of power, it would disparage those rights which were not singled out, were intended to be assigned the Federal Government and were consequently insecure. This is one of the most plausible arguments I have ever heard against the admission of a bill of rights into the system; but I conceive, that it may be guarded against... (Page 439)

> Mr. Jackson... There is a maxim in law, and it will apply to the Bill of Rights, that when you enumerate exceptions, the exceptions operate to the exclusion of all circumstances that are noted; consequently unless you except every right from the grant of power, those omitted are inferred to be resigned to the discretion of the Federal Government... (Page 441)

In practice, the Federal Government has not voided the old rule of law and is doing all it can to subvert and illegally take away unlisted rights from one group of people and arbitrarily give it to another. Particularly in Roe vs. Wade, the Court manipulated these unlisted rights and declared rights not in the U.S. Constitution.

The San Jose City Council did this also, in the most blatant manner seen for at least a decade, in order to stop lawful protests outside of charnel houses in that city. All such decisions by courts and by local and state authorities, to pass restrictive ordinances against the rights of citizens to protest and to bear arms, are a violation of the 9th Amendment and the 2nd Amendment and are thus, without exception, null and void.

Unlisted rights and privileges found in State constitutions include the following:

➤ The right to a birth certificate.

➤ The privilege of an eighth-grade certificate.

Incidentally, education is not a right, but a privilege and comes under the privileges and immunities clause of Article IV, Section II, part 1 of the Constitution.

➤ The privilege of a high school certificate.

➤ The right of a marriage certificate.

➤ The right of a death certificate and a decent Christian burial.

➤ The privilege to attend law school, college or other higher learning institutions.

➤ The right to travel or go from one place to another, freely and without restrictions.

➤ The right to travel to foreign nations.

➤ The right under the U.S. Constitution to keep government as small as possible and to be free of excessive government bureaucracy.

➤ The right to stay away from government as much as possible.

> ➤ The right to come and go, and do what one wants to do in life.

> ➤ The right to decide how many children a married couple may have.

These are just a few examples of the un-enumerated rights, and the rights that are not enumerated do not mean that it is legal to have an abortion. The Supreme Court was wrong in exercising predilection in deciding Roe vs. Wade, and it is a very serious error. The domino effect of that incorrect ruling has been that local and state authorities now try to lessen the rights of those who are seeking to protest wholesale murder at abortion "clinics," which is patently unconstitutional.

On page 2286 of pages 2273-2297, Congressional Record, House, February 26, 1990, it is clearly spelled out:

> The 9th Amendment to the U.S. Constitution expressly states the existence of other rights which are retained by the people and that these rights shall not be denied or disparaged because certain express rights are enumerated in the Constitution or its amendments.

The owners and operators and those who perform "services" in the charnel houses are the ones violating the U.S. Constitution and Bill of Rights, as are local governments like the San Jose City Council.

A city's police force, in enforcing such an unconstitutional ordinance, is in violation of the U.S. Constitution. Have you ever noticed how these lawbreakers try to cover their intent with flowery semantics? They call themselves "health providers" and their establishments "clinics."

They talk about "women's reproductive rights" and "family planning" and call their organizations by a variety of names such as The Coalition of Our Reproductive Rights, Women's Rights Activists and so on. Never do they call themselves abortionists.

6

ABORTION HOUSES ARE NOT CLINICS

Let us examine the meaning of the word "clinic:" From the Greek word, klinikus, pertaining to the bed; bedridden.

- ➢ The teaching of medicine by examining and training patients in the presence of students.

- ➢ A class getting such teaching.

- ➢ A place where patients are studied or treated by physicians specializing in various ailments and practicing as a group; as a cancer clinic; a tuberculosis clinic.

- ➢ The dispensary or outpatients department of a hospital, or medical school, where patients are treated free or for a small fee.

- ➢ An organization or institution that offers some kind of advice / treatment, such as a domestic-relations clinic.

- ➢ A brief, intensive session of group instruction in a specific skill, field of knowledge etc.; as a basketball clinic.

(*Webster's New Universal Unabridged Dictionary*) It would be interesting to file a legal brief against the charnel house operators for deceptive practices, for there is nothing in the above definition of a clinic that would allow an abortion mill be classed as a "clinic" or to be established as a business under this title. There appears to be a contradiction in legal terms if such abortion mills apply for a business license under the title of a "clinic." Could this be characterized as deceptive practice? perhaps it is an avenue worth exploring?

It is doubtful that in Roe vs. Wade the Supreme Court Judges read Volume III of Judge Story's volumes on the U.S. Constitution on chapter interpretation; if the judges had made any kind of a study of this famous work by Judge Story, Roe vs. Wade would have been consigned to the dumpsters where, instead, the mangled bodies of murdered infants are now thrown:

> In the first place, then, every word employed in the constitution is to be explained in its plain, obvious, and commons sense, unless the context furnishes some ground to control, qualify or enlarge it. Constitutions are not designed for metaphysical or logical subtleties (as in Roe vs. Wade), for niceties of expression, for critical propriety, for elaborate shades of meaning, or the exercise of philosophical acuteness, or judicial research.

> They are instruments of a practical nature, founded on the common business of human life, adapted to common wants, designed for common use, and fitted for common understandings. The people make them; the people are supposed to read them, with the help of common sense; and cannot be presumed to admit in them any recondite meaning or extraordinary gloss...

> (Pages 436-437 Part 451, XV)

Judge Story dealt at length with the 9th Amendment and stated:

The enumeration in the Constitution shall not be construed to deny or disparage others retained by the people...

The maxim, rightly understood, is perfectly sound and safe; but it has often been strangely forced from its natural meaning into the support of the most dangerous 45 political heresies. The amendment was undoubtedly suggested by the reasoning of the Federalists on the subject of a general bill of rights.

If ever there is a perfect of example of the maxim "presumed to admit in them any recondite meaning" and being "strangely forced from its natural meaning into the support of the most dangerous political heresies," that example is clearly found in Roe vs. Wade.

The political Leftist Socialist incendiaries were able to work the Communist Manifesto of 1848 into so-called "civil rights," which they translated into "abortion rights."

Although the 9th Amendment was aimed particularly at the judiciary, all local, state and federal officials are bound by it.

There are so many Leftist, Liberal and Socialist-Communists in Congress that Supreme Court judges were able, with their support, to force the 9th Amendment from its natural meaning, in order to twist and squeeze abortion rights into the Constitution and Bill of Rights where it does not belong and does not exist.

These incendiary Liberal-Leftist-Fabian Socialists have also somehow, by displaying a remarkable skill in contortion, bluffed Americans into accepting "equal rights" and equating this with "abortion rights."

What the Supreme Court did in Roe vs. Wade was to impose recondite, esoteric, abstruse meanings, philosophical acuteness, elaborate shades of meaning, all manner of the product of uncontrollable figments of imagination.

The U.S. Supreme Court in Roe vs. Wade tried to combine the Communist Manifesto of 1848 with the U.S. Constitution. The Court seriously compromised the Constitution.

From the very beginning, Roe vs. Wade was outside the pale and ken of the U.S. Constitution where it should have remained, as abortion rights are nowhere found in the U.S. Constitution and the Bill of Rights.

Thomas Jefferson was fully aware of the dangers of mixing politics with the judiciary. If he were alive today, he would recoil in horror over the behavior of the Socialist-Fabianist influence at work in the Senate Labor Subcommittee and the Senate Judiciary Committee, where candidates for the Supreme Court have to satisfy political considerations of the far left before they can pass these supposed watchdogs of We, the People.

In a letter to Dr. Thomas Richie dated Dec. 25, 1820, Jefferson expressed his concern over a future Supreme Court:

> The judiciary of the United States is the subtle corps of sappers and miners constantly working underground to undermine the foundations of our confederated fabric.

They are construing our Constitution from a coordination of a general and special government to general and supreme one alone. This will lay all things at their feet, and they are too well versed in English law to forget the maxim boni judicis est ampliare jurisdiction.

A judiciary independent of a king or executive is a good thing; but independence of the will of the nation is a solecism, at least in a Republican government.

In a letter to the Honorable M. Coray dated Oct. 31, 1823, Thomas Jefferson expressed his fear of the judiciary getting out of hand as follows:

... At the establishment of our Constitution, the judiciary bodies were supposed to be the most helpless and harmless, however, they soon showed in which way they 47 were to become the most dangerous; that the insufficiency of the means for their removal gave them a freehold irresponsibility in office; that their decisions, seemingly to concern individual suitors only, pass silently and unheeded by the public at large; that these decisions nevertheless, become law by precedent; sapping, by construction before anyone has perceived that invisible worm has been busily employed in consuming its substance. In truth man is not made to be trusted for life, if secured against all liability to account...

Then again on Jan. 19th 1821, Washington wrote to a Mr. C. Hammond about his fears of the judiciary:

... It has long, however, been my opinion, and I have never shrunk from its expression (although I do not choose to put it in a newspaper, or like a Priam in armor offer myself as its champion), that the germ of dissolution of our Federal Government is in the constitution of the Federal judiciary;

... an irresponsible body (for impeachment is scarcely a scarecrow), working like gravity, by night and by day, gaining a little today and a little tomorrow, advancing its noiseless step like a thief over the field of jurisdiction, until all shall be usurped from the State and the government, domestic and foreign, in little as in great things, shall be drawn to Washington as the center of all power, and it will render powerless the checks provided of one government on another, and will become as venal and oppressive as the government from which we have separated, it will be as in Europe, where every man must be pikes or gudgeon hammer or anvil.

If the States look with apathy on this silent descent of their Government into the gulf which is to swallow us all, we have only to weep over the human character found 48 uncontrollable but by a rod of iron and the blasphemers of man as incapable of self-government became its true historians.

If ever the Constitution was blasphemed it was in the 1973 Supreme Court ruling on Roe vs. Wade.

How much do our representatives and senators know about the Constitution? The answer is that the majority of them are woefully ignorant of it, if the way their leaders operate is any judge of their competency. In any event, apart from some notable exceptions, most of our legislators are incendiary light-as-air liberals, or else under the domination of the Socialists.

Some of those who control the Socialists would have made Lenin and Stalin look like novices when it comes to pushing the Marxist-Leninist-Fabian Socialist agenda. A concrete example of what I am talking about is the legislation proposed by Former Senator George Mitchell, then Democrat majority leader in the Senate.

Unlike Abraham Lincoln who studied the Constitution for many years before entering politics, Mitchell's knowledge of the Constitution is obviously limited if one uses his Bill S25 to judge his competency.

During the 19th century, it was expressly implied that every Congressman had studied the Constitution for at least two years, or how else could they have sworn to uphold it if they did not know what the Constitution contained? And I am not talking about taking a course by some "Eastern Liberal Establishment" far-left, Marxist-Socialist professor and lover of the Communist Manifesto of 1848.

Here is how Mitchell showed his ignorance of the Constitution:

> S25, a bill to protect the reproduction rights of women, and for other purposes, to the Committee on Labor ana Human Resources.

This is found on page S427 of pages S426-431, Congressional Record, Senate January 21, 1993. The first thing to note is the false and misleading title of the bill. The second thing to note is that the Senate Committee of Labor and Human Resources is as far left as one can go without packing one's bags and departing for Moscow.

The "big three" at that time were Senators Kennedy, Metzenbaum and Simon, who dominated its proceedings and went outside of and beyond the pale of the US Constitution when it comes to any decision-making. One wonders how these three Fabian Socialists were appointed to this key Committee. The title of this bill is a cheap, tawdry slogan adopted by those who favor the Communist Manifesto of 1848, "freedom of choice," also known as "free love without responsibility."

Let us examine the contention of Fabian-Socialist Mitchell: Privacy is not the only un-enumerated right; the right of citizens to associate freely with each other is nowhere mentioned in the Constitution.

> ➤ The right of Americans to travel is not specified in the Constitution.
> ➤ The right to marry is not spelled out.
> ➤ Neither is the right to have children.

But no one denies that these rights are fundamental rights of every American.

In Roe vs. Wade, the Supreme Court said that the right of privacy is broad enough to encompass a woman's decision whether or not to terminate her privacy. That finding is what my bill seeks to uphold, no more, no less.

What Mitchell showed is that he does not know the difference between personal rights and constitutional rights and he got them all mixed up. No matter how much Mitchell and his fellow liberal incendiaries tried to fit the Constitution to their goals, there is not the remotest connection here between so-called right of privacy and abortion.

Abortion is a crime against Natural Law, and was so stated in almost all 50 States until Roe vs. Wade.

Let us suppose that there is a law stating that a man between the ages of 18 and 21 is not a man, but only partly a man. Would that be accepted? Yet, this is what Roe vs. Wade has done; it negates the 5th Amendment and no legislation can ever set aside the Constitution.

Persons and citizens are identical. To attempt to draw a distinction between the unborn baby in the womb and to call this baby-child a citizen-person only at birth, is the height of ridiculous inanity ever dreamed.

Life begins at conception, but the incendiary abortionists attempt to get by this road block by calling the unborn child a "fetus" so as to disguise what is essentially, in plain language, murder.

7

ABORTION IS "CRUEL AND UNUSUAL PUNISHMENT"

A bortion metes out "cruel and unusual punishment" to the most defenseless of all citizens. If the power to murder babies is granted in the Constitution, it would only be found in Article 1, Section 8, Clause 1-18 in the enumerated powers of Congress. Moreover, Congress has no absolute power under the U.S. Constitution.

Congress cannot legislate abortion rights, when it is a prohibition of that right in the Constitution, and in any case by legislating abortion Congress would be violating the 10th Amendment as the Supreme Court did in Roe vs. Wade.

I would have welcomed the opportunity to ask Senators Mitchell, Metzenbaum, Kennedy, Simon, Sarbanes, Boxer, Feinstein and every other incendiary liberal in the Senate and the Supreme Court Justices, to prove that the right to murder babies is contained in the said Clauses 1-18. There is not a power that is remotely expressed or implied here to commit such sadistic, barbarous cruelty of which not even primitive, savage nations are guilty.

"Well," say the incendiaries, "what about clause 18 itself?"

Clause 18 is the only power in which the House and Senate have the freedom of an implied power.

As I said earlier, the clause allows Congress and the Senate to make all laws which shall be necessary and proper, and I would like anyone from the ranks of the Socialists — and the Supreme Court — to show cause why it is "necessary and proper" to murder babies.

In addition to being "necessary and proper," any such power taken has to be expressly implied or related to a power already in the Constitution.

As there is no expressed or implied power in the Constitution, Clause 18 could not be invoked to cover abortion.

When the Constitution is silent on a power and it is not incidental to another power, it is a prohibition of that power.

When the U.S. Supreme Court goes beyond the strict confines of the Constitution as it did in Roe vs. Wade and the "Gun Control" Bill of 1968, then such decisions or laws, statues or local ordinances have no force and they are outside of the pale and the ken of Constitution and therefore illegal.

The plain fact is that there is no provision in the Constitution for abortion. Free love, or Roe vs. Wade, is a Communists Manifesto of 1848 "interpretation" of the Constitution and the Bill of Rights. One of the few in Congress who knew the Constitution was former Rep. Robert Dornan, (who lost his seat through possible election fraud) and here is what he said on this false Roe vs. Wade ruling:

> ... And speaking of Roe vs. Wade, a lying case on a rape that never happened, Norma McCovey is running around

this country with her radical feminist friends, the NARL people and the NOW people, still talking about how she should have been allowed to abort all three of her daughters, and guess what, her daughters are still alive in their twenties...

Congressional Record, House, page H6656, September 17th 1991.

Norma McCovey was untruthful in Roe vs. Wade. There was no rape. Why didn't McCovey give her real name in the case? Why 53 did she hide behind a false name? This alone, should have been sufficient cause for Roe vs. Wade not to be taken up by the Supreme Court, but to its everlasting shame, the Court did it under duress from the incendiary Marxist-Leninist-Communist-Fabian Socialists who control the media and the House and Senate.

Norma McCovey told an untruth and should be branded as an untruthful person, especially as she now tells another lie to compound the first, namely that illegal abortion was rampant before Roe vs. Wade. Where is McCovey's proof of this? The plain answer is that she had none. But since Roe vs. Wade, abortion has become rampant - what the Communist Manifesto of 1848 dreamed of accomplishing has come to pass. Anarchy reigns in this country.

"Rights without Responsibility" is the battle cry of McCovey and the radicals of NOW and NARL. "Long live Communism and the Family, Long Live Alexandra Kollontei," cry the equivalent of the Paris mobs of the French Revolution; only now their cry is not "death to the Aristos," but "death to infants."

These radical feminist Marxist-Communist lovers of the Communist Manifesto of 1848 don't need a guillotine; any charnel house masquerading as a "clinic" will dispatch the unborn child. "To hell with Dannemeyer" they cry, "who needs restraint."

Former Representative William Dannemeyer once posed the question from the floor of the House; "What is wrong with restraint? Women have a responsibility to be restrained, for without restraint, the nation will be buried under a tidal wave of anarchy," exactly the aims of the Communist Manifesto of 1848.

To the loud chorus of approval from the selected, elected left wing incendiaries in the Senate, Mitchell plowed ahead with his bill, cheered on by Senators Kennedy, Metzenbaum, Simon, Sarbanes, Boxer, Wellstone and Biden, plus the whole Collectivist-Socialist group in the Senate. In Senator Mitchell we have a prime example of a Senator who should know the Constitution, yet we find him writing a bill in total ignorance of natural law and the Constitution. In this instance, the rights of marriage, to have children and to travel etc. are personal rights and congressmen and senators listed them as such in the 19th century in the Congressional Record.

What has happened in the interim is that these rights have been stolen from the American people by judges and their incendiary liberal backers like Kennedy, Metzenbaum and Simon. They did this in the 1950s when they passed so-called "race laws," which they dubbed "civil rights," all of which laws are unconstitutional.

The only civil right that is constitutional is found in the 5th Amendment:

> ... Nor to be deprived of life, liberty and property without due process of law...

The 14th and 15th Amendments were never constitutionally ratified by the States, as anyone who takes the trouble to read the Reconstruction debates will surely discover.

I venture to suggest that 90 percent of congressmen and senators have not studied the Reconstruction debates otherwise they would never have supported liberal incendiary-socialists Mitchell's faux pas.

The U.S. Supreme Court cannot make laws, except on a case-by-case basis, and even then the legislative body has to consider the motion to approve it, before it can become law.

It is an absurdity to believe that one set of circumstances in a case before the Supreme Court can somehow apply to the entire nation. I will go further and say it is stupid.

Because they believe they can draw unconstitutional support from the House and Senate, city councils all across the nation are passing a welter of ordinances, which presume to inhibit the right of free speech and the right of assembly, and the right to bear arms. In their zeal to advance the cause of mass murder of infants, and to limit protest and to abolish the right to bear arms, the Marxist-Leninist-Fabian Socialists attempt to abridge the rights of We, the People.

> There shall be no law respecting the establishment of religion, or prohibiting the free exercise thereof; habeas corpus is not to be suspended; Freedom of speech is not to be abridged; The right to assemble and petition for redress of grievances and the right to keep and bear arms shall not be abridged.

The City Council of San Jose was obviously wrong in attempting to put local laws above the Constitution, it hastily threw together ordinances to stop those who abhor the mass slaughter of infants taking place in their county, from exercising their constitutional right to protest child murder. Also, we need to look again at the 10th Amendment which states:

> The powers not delegated to the United States by the Constitution, nor prohibited by it to the States, are reserved to the States, or to the people.

This means that the delegated powers given to the Federal Government and those powers left over which apply to the State Constitution are reserved to the people.

We need to understand that in the words "or to the people" is found a large number of rights called personal rights that are constantly being encroached upon by State, local and Federal Government under the guise of "equal rights, "gun control" and "civil rights," not to mention so-called "affirmative action" laws.

I have not seen anything much written about or spoken about by Congress and the courts concerning these rights since the 19th century. These inalienable rights have been swept under the rug and forgotten. The U.S. Constitution and the Bill of Rights are based on common law (Natural Law).

When the original States adopted the Constitution, they were permitted to keep their common law, but some of that common law has been subverted, which can be traced to Marxist-Leninist-Fabian Socialist Franklin D. Roosevelt, who began packing the Supreme Court with lovers of the Communist Manifesto. It was in the Roosevelt era that strenuous attempts were made to unify and simplify State laws (common law.) There is not a single word in the Constitution that granted power to Socialist Franklin D. Roosevelt to make uniform or to simplify common law. That was a goal of the Communist Manifesto of 1848.

As Daniel Webster once stated, any attempts to simplify the U.S. Constitution leads to autocracy or loss of freedoms. Webster stated that our liberties are in the complexities of the U.S. Constitution and Amendments and Bill of Rights. Webster foresaw what the Marxist-Leninist-Fabian Socialists would try to do.

In 1920, in the vanguard of an assault by the Fabians, the activists tried to get a uniform textbook forced on Oregon schools, but they were thwarted. Uniform textbooks will indoctrinate our children into believing in a Socialist One World Government quicker than most other methods. Roe vs. Wade falls within the same orbit; in fact not only should this case have not gone to court, it should never have been taken up by the Supreme Court, based solely upon the fact that McCovey lied and continued to lie, even in front of the Supreme Court, not to mention the strictures of the 10th Amendment.

There is another set of rights which apply that makes abortion illegal which is not found in inalienable law.

Unhappily, the Founding Fathers never foresaw that the people of the country would be brainwashed into wholesale murder of their own infants, so they were somewhat short on inalienable rights as we find in Article IV, Section 2 and Clause 1 of the U.S.

Constitution:

> The citizens of each State shall be entitled to all privilege of citizens in several States.

Take careful note that it does not say the laws have to be uniform in each State; the only requirement is that they achieve the same results.

These rights are not guaranteed by the Constitution. The privileges and immunities apply to serving on a jury, to voting and to holding public office, although public office is not among them.

On pages 280-288, Appendix to the Congressional Record, May 20, 1908, is found an excellent treatise by George Gray and the Honorable John S. Williams, which makes the connection between privileges and rights, which should have been more efficiently spelled out by the Founding Fathers. Nowhere in the treatise is found the faintest hint or resemblance to a "right" to abortion.

Thomas Jefferson spoke to the question of rights in the Declaration of Independence, but, unfortunately, this was not included in the U.S. Constitution; the U.S. Constitution should have been written around the Declaration of

Independence; had that happened it would have prevented baby-murder and foiled the abortionist in plying his or her evil trade.

In writing this book, I have a tremendous advantage over lawyers, the Justice Department, senators and congressman. Lawyers have about one semester on the Constitution - perish the thought!

They do not ever study the Congressional Record, which is where I found all of my information, and there is no better place to get it. Had the Supreme Court justices searched the Congressional Record, there would be no such insanity as Roe vs. Wade today.

One cannot turn to the radio, television, computer, or open the newspaper, without being bludgeoned by some commentator/reporter who can barely keep the joy from his or her face or from their editorials that another round for "freedom of choice" (free love without responsibility) has been won in the courts. Congresswoman Bella Sisisky Abzug in her hey-day was a natural megaphone for such inanities — her fog horn voice never stopped bellowing across the land, the message "death to infants."

Never mind the fact that there is nothing in the U.S. Constitution that allows for child murder; that only made Alexandra Kollontei-lover Abzug bellow all the louder.

For abortion to be legal it would take an amendment to the U.S. Constitution, ratified by all 50 of the States. The U.S. Constitution as it stands is silent on abortion, which means it is a prohibition of abortion. Serious students of the Constitution should read the Congressional Record for the past fifty years; better yet, go back 200 years — which would help them to grasp what is happening to the Constitution today.

I stress that I am not a lawyer nor am I "practicing law." The information I have provided is taken from records in the public domain which are available to all.

After 35 years of mass-murder of babies, 2009 finds the Democrat Party leadership still shuffling its feet, still trying to sweep this, the most important constitutional issue ever to arise in the history of the country, under the carpet.

8

REPUBLICANS DO CARPET SHUFFLE OVER ABORTION

At the Republican National Convention meeting held at Palm Springs in 1984, they did the carpet shuffle all over again. Instead of facing the issue, the Republican Party tried to play down the importance of the abortion issue.

The Republican Corporate Board Room Club ($100,000 per member) calls the issue "divisive" — that's all - and demands "unity" meaning those rank and file members of the party who hate abortion must pipe down and join the "mainstream opinion."

If those heroes of our nation who refused to "join the mainstream" at the time when only three percent of them were prepared to take up arms and fight against King George III had not rejected the "mainstream" call, where would our nation be today?

The Republican Board Room Club says abortion is a medical problem which must be treated like any other medical problem.

Why are they saying this? First, because they are afraid of losing their financial hold over the party, which enables them to continue to receive the favors they have paid for, and secondly, it is apparent that they neither know nor care anything about the Constitutional issues at stake here.

This attitude makes them no different from the Democrat Party which has largely closed ranks on the abortion issue and is no longer talking about a "tent big enough to cover all shades of opinion." When Chairman of the Christian Right Tim Lambert and his men were brave enough to call for withholding party funds from candidates who would not come out and openly take a stand against abortion, he was told:

We are all against abortion but we have to keep our rhetoric down lest we frighten away the moderates, and we need their votes in the House and Senate.

As Lambert pointed out:

> I didn't hear any screams of "litmus test" or "big tent" or "slippery slope" when the RNC refused to fund David Duke's candidacy.

Of course not! It was not "politically correct" to support Duke, and it is not "politically correct" to support moves to end the butchery of Roe vs. Wade. The Republican National Committee (RNC) wants to be all things to all men, so they tell their rank and file, "look, just get our people elected and then we can turn to the business of saving little babies."

Sounds fine on the surface, but those candidates the RNC want to get elected won't support a ban on Roe vs. Wade. Look what happened in the primaries in Santa Barbara in 1988.

Liberal candidate Brooks Firestone (heir to the Firestone Tire Company fortune and the candidate-of-choice of the RNC) would not state his position on abortion and Mr. Firestone is the type of candidate that Henry Hyde and the RNC want to have in the Congress.

Instead of Firestone getting the nomination, a virtually unknown grass roots candidate, Tom Bordonaro, beat out Firestone and Lois Capps, a liberal Democrat who favored abortion. Bordonaro won because he said exactly what he meant and made known his fierce opposition to abortion. That is the kind of candidate the Republican Party needs, nothing below the standard of candidate Bordonaro will do.

Bordonaro won in spite of a dirty tricks campaign waged against him by three local Santa Barbara television stations, which first agreed to air his advertisements, and then reneged on their promise. The stations said they were afraid of breaking Federal Communication Commission (FCC) laws if they displayed graphic photos of children murdered by abortion, and so they sought refuge behind FCC regulations which did not apply.

These terrified liberals did not want the public to get a graphic view of the handiwork of the abortion mill-charnel houses operating in the Santa Barbara area and elsewhere across the country. So they ran to the FCC and said in effect,

> "... look, we want to keep to our agreement to air Bordonaro's ads, but we are afraid if we do so, we will fall foul of the indecency law because we think that the Bordonaro ads show a by-product of an excretory activity; a fetus from the uterus."

No wonder I have always referred to the media as "jackals" and this is a case in point which seems to me to justify the epithet.

The objection by these three cowardly television stations was nothing but mendacity, sophistry, venal platitudes and outright lying. In the end not even the FCC could stomach the station's point of view, but by that time the election was over.

The FCC I might add, broke its own rules in accommodating a hearing of the three television stations' appeal, because in September 1996, a Federal Appeals Court ruled that "Content-based channeling of indecent political advertising" (which rule did not include photos of mangled babies — the court called these murdered babies, fetuses), are a violation of the Communications Act of 1934.

"Channeling" is a device where indecent and objectionable material can be screened, but only after so-called "safe harbor" hours which in plain language means very late at night or the early hours of the morning.

The three Santa Barbara stations knew very well their claim that photos of aborted babies did not come under the heading of 62 "indecent material" was bogus, but their fraudulent case successfully delayed candidate Bordonaro's adds from being screened during the election. The stations knew very well that the FCC definition of indecency was "any patently offensive portrayal of sexual or execratory activity or organs."

So the defense put up by the three television stations that "by this definition the abortion commercials were indecent because they show a by-product of excretory activity from a uterus," was patently and grossly absurd. All women ought to be highly offended by the "pro-life" crowd equating the birth of a child to excreting fecal matter, and so should all men everywhere, that the miracle of birth can be so degraded by the "pro-life" groups.

What the abortionists and their political Communist allies fear the most is a full political discussion about the total unconstitutionality of abortion and the evil it does to the morality of the nation. The Republican Party plays right into the hands of the abortionists by trying to stifle full and free debate at its national meetings and other gatherings.

"Don't let us divide the party by focusing on this single issue," their leaders said. "There is plenty of room under our 'big tent' for all shades of opinion on this issue." That leaves unanswered the question of how in the name of God can the people be properly informed about what is going on with abortion, when the major party supposed to be against abortion, refuses to speak out boldly, loudly, without any apologies for being against child murder, the product of "free love?"

The pro-child murder groups, which include the majority of the Democrat Party's ruling hierarchy, speak out loudly and frequently. They don't mind going as far as saying, "well, there is some use for an unwanted child — only they say "fetus." Take the letter written by Rep. Nancy Pelosi, a Bay Area Democrat, and which was published by the ultra-leftist San Francisco Chronicle on the 25th anniversary of Roe vs. Wade.

Pelosi has now graduated to the leadership of the Congress, but in my opinion, unless she is willing to revoke her pro-abortion stance, she has no place in the legislature and that applies to all members of the House and Senate who favor abortion. How can they swear an oath to uphold the Constitution and then flagrantly trample it underfoot by favoring murder of the unborn child?

... The majority of Americans support the right to make reproductive decisions free from government interference. Yet a relentless anti-choice minority represented by the most solidly anti-choice Congress since the Roe vs. Wade decision, is determined to eliminate access to abortion by whatever means... Knowing that public opinion is firmly on the side of the right to choose, these forces have been restricting access to abortion coverage for federal employees...

Family planning services save the lives and health of young women and children here and in developing countries... The prohibition for fetal tissue and human embryo research stifles the possibility of finding treatments for conditions such as cancer, Alzheimers disease, juvenile diabetes and infertility...

The rest of Congresswoman Pelosi's letter was a tearful plea for those against child murder to stop opposition to the "right" to murder infant children. Now, this is not just a member of the public writing. This was a well-respected member of the House. As such one would imagine that Pelosi knew the U.S. Constitution and the Bill of Rights, but her letter indicates otherwise: Pelosi uses the word "rights" or "right" throughout her letter. There is no such right found in the Constitution that would allow abortion.

Justice Blackmun found a provision in the Constitution, which as Sam Ervin said "... is not there."

By a most profound stretch of his vivid imagination, Blackmun declared that the 4th Amendment was "broad enough" for a woman to have an abortion.

Through his warped decision, Blackmun violated the 5th, 9th and 10th Amendments and for that he should have been removed from the court. For Pelosi's information the only rights listed in the Constitution are:

> ➢ The right to keep and bear arms (which Pelosi strongly opposes).
> ➢ The right to the protection of life, liberty and property.

There are un-enumerated personal rights which the Congress never talks about these days, and it appears that Pelosi is all scrambled up and mixes personal rights with constitutional rights. Notwithstanding that personal rights do not cover murder of the unborn.

As Professor Arthur Miller of the Harvard Law School said at the time the Court handed down its Roe vs. Wade ruling:

> The Supreme Court found a right of abortion without pointing to any specific word in the Constitution.

In other words there is NO provision for abortion in the Constitution.

Justice Byron White of the Supreme Court said:

I find nothing in the language of history of the Constitution to support the court's judgment.

So from whence does the "right" of abortion come from? Pelosi repeats the unproven claim that the majority of the American people support abortion. Pelosi bases her invalid claim on statistical sampling. There is no constitutional authority in the U.S. Constitution for statistical sampling, also known as "polling" as a basis for a constitutional power. The U.S. Constitution has no power to make laws based on polling.

What the Constitution says is that matters of constitutional moment must be referred to the voters in the States in a form of an amendment to the Constitution. If Pelosi and her supporters are so confident that the vast majority of Americans are for abortion "rights," then let the matter be debated in the Congress and voted upon and the result put to the States in its proper form as a referendum. This was denied to the people of the States by the Supreme Court and on this point alone, Roe vs. Wade must be overturned.

Mr. Justice Byron White who dissented said:

> The upshot (of Roe vs. Wade) is that the people of the legislatures of the 50 States were disentitled to weigh the relative importance of the fetus on the one hand against a spectrum of possible impacts on the mother on the other hand. As an exercise of raw judicial power, the court perhaps has authority to do what it does today but in my view its judgment is an improvident and extravagant exercise of the power of judicial review which the Constitution extends to the courts.

Although he was on the right track, Justice Byron White erred in several respects; mainly in talking about a "fetus" and by saying that the court, "perhaps has the authority to do what it does today." Roe vs. Wade is no more than a cheap, sordid, underhand trick to deny the unborn child citizenship under the 5th Amendment. Vattel's Law of Nations, the "Bible" upon which our Founding Fathers relied in drafting the Constitution, puts the matter beyond dispute and forever smashes the Communist Manifesto interpretation of the 1973 Supreme Court Roe vs. Wade ruling.

Vattel's Law of Nations, pages 478-479:

> The citizens are members of the civil society bound to the society by certain duties and subject to its authority; they actually participate in its advantages ... As a society cannot perpetuate itself otherwise than by children, they (children) naturally follow the condition of their parents and succeed to all their rights.

"Freedom of choice" is a gruesome farce. The baby in the womb "follows the condition of the parents and succeeds to all of their rights."

How cowardly to destroy a helpless, unborn child. There is not one single word in the Constitution and the Bill of Rights nor is it anywhere expressly implied that a women has the "constitutional right" to abortion. For this reason alone, abortion is not a "right," but an abomination of desolation.

The man who started the cult of abortion, Justice Harry Blackmun had his wish granted: "I will carry Roe vs. Wade to my grave," Blackmun said. This is the unconstitutional lawyer who found the right of abortion in the Constitution where it did not exist. To critics who challenged him on his abortion finding, Blackmun said:

> ... The Constitution does not explicitly mention any right to privacy, but it is broad enough to encompass a women's decision whether or not to terminate her pregnancy.

What Blackmun did was to read his own thoughts on abortion into the Constitution. This is known as predilection, and predilection is forbidden to judges. They cannot read what they want to be in the Constitution as if it were there. This is exactly what liberal Harry Blackmun did. Worse still, Harry Blackmun was proud of defiling the Constitution. In some of his gloating speeches before his liberal colleagues and friends, he boasted that his Roe vs. Wade ruling had caused great distress among Christians, which he said was a source of pleasure for him. While masquerading as a conservative in order to get elected to the Supreme Court, Blackmun was in reality acting as a committed Socialist. He claimed to be a Republican but was not. He claimed to be a conservative just long enough to be elevated to the Supreme Court, after which his "conservatism" underwent a remarkably rapid conversion to ultra-liberal liberalism.

Of Blackmun's contorted predilection, Justice Byron White wrote in his dissenting opinion:

> I find nothing in the language of the history of the Constitution to support the court's judgment. The court simply fashions a new constitutional right for pregnant mothers with scarcely any reason or authority for its action invests the right without sufficient substance to override more State abortion statutes.

Blackmun was the evil abettor who opened the door to butchery of human babies and fashioned his ersatz conservative label out of his support for the death penalty, and in this manner deceived those gullible senators, who confirmed his appointment to the Supreme Court.

In 1992 Blackmun ran up his personal Red Flag to the mast of liberalism in his dissent in the Callins case, in which a convicted murderer, Bruce Callins was sentenced to death. Apparently this infidel thought he had the right to decide who shall die and who shall live.

"Kill babies, but don't put a convicted murderer to death" is what he said in so many words.

In the Callins case, Blackmun wrote:

> I feel morally and intellectually obligated to simply concede that the death penalty experiment has failed. From this day forward I no longer tinker with the machinery of death.

Such astounding hypocrisy deserves a monument to its dishonor.

While Blackmun felt morally obligated to rule that millions of babies could be murdered under some non-existent constitutional provision - solely the conjecturing of his fevered, Socialist mind - he did not feel morally obligated to allow the State to put convicted murderer Bruce Callins to death.

This judge with a weirdly contorted mind felt that upholding the death penalty was to "tinker with the machinery of death," while the murder of millions of innocent babies was no more than "a right to privacy" not found in the 4th Amendment to the Constitution.

There is not one single word in the Constitution and the Bill of Rights, nor is it anywhere expressly implied, that women have a constitutional right to abortion.

9

ROE vs. WADE: A POWER NOT FOUND IN THE U.S. CONSTITUTION

The late Senator Sam Ervin, who knew a thing or two about the Constitution, said of Blackmun's predilection:

> In Roe vs. Wade, the Supreme Court found something that is not in the Constitution.

Not content with trashing the Constitution once, Blackmun discovered yet another non-existent provision in the Constitution — the "right" to commit acts of sodomy under the same stretched 4th Amendment "right to privacy." What a ridiculous statement to come from the Supreme Court.

The Constitution cannot be stretched to fit the predilections of judges — the 9th Amendment forbids it. The Supreme Court judges who backed Blackmun should have been impeached and removed from office on the grounds of legislating when they knew full well that the power to make laws resides solely with the Congress.

In the case of Bowers vs. Hardwick, this mixed-up bench warmer decreed that the "most comprehensive of rights and the right most valued by civilized men" was privacy.

Here again, Blackmun inserted his fevered thinking between the lines of the Constitution just as he did in Roe vs. Wade and somehow included homosexuality, shunned by all civilized men down through the ages, under the umbrella of the 4th Amendment.

In the full grip of his "intellectual" predilection frenzy, Blackmun dredged up homosexual rights where there were none before:

> The fact that individuals define themselves in a significant way through their intimate sexual relationships with each other, suggests, in a nation as diverse as ours, that there may be many "right" ways of conducting those relationships.

Thus did the man who opened the door to butchery of babies find the "right" way to give homosexuals constitutional rights as a class when no such rights have ever existed and still do not exist?

What this strange man Blackmun did not appear to know is that morals cannot be legislated. No one can create out of fresh air, legislation that treats sodomy as a special right and makes the sodomist a special class of citizen. In one fell swoop, Blackmun attempted to set aside 2000 years of Christian civilization and the United States Constitution. He ruled abortion legal in total violation of Christian principles and a gross violation of the U.S. Constitution.

The "right" to abortion does not exist in the Constitution or the Bill of Rights. The people of this nation must be marshaled to defend the unborn child from murder and mayhem. If we do not oppose with all our Christian faith this Bogomil and Cathar doctrine, the United States will surely go the way of Rome and Greece.

Congressional Record, House, July 3, 1926, page 12942:

> It (the Communist Manifesto of 1848) has expressly abolished, prohibited all rights of inheritance, whether by law or by will... they have promulgated decrees relating to marriage and to divorce which practically establishes a state of 'free love' (abortion). Their effect has been to furnish a vehicle for the legalizing of prostitution by permitting annulment of the marriage bonds at the whim of the parties.

> Abortion is the most important issue in the history of the United States. Those who would stand aside from it are committing a grave error and delivering a cowardly blow against the Republic of the United States of America and its institutions by which we will stand or fall. What is the solution?

We, the People, must petition the Congress to overturn the unconstitutional Supreme Court ruling known as Roe vs. Wade.

We have the right to take such action and the Congress has the right to overturn Roe vs. Wade and its attendant rulings under Article III, Section 2, Part 2, and it would only take a simple majority, not a two-thirds majority vote, to accomplish it. Let us therefore proceed along these constitutional lines and eschew violence against the murderers of our defenseless infants.

PRESIDENT OBAMA FAVORS ABORTION

President Barack Obama's views on life issues ranging from abortion to embryonic stem cell research mark him as not merely "pro-abortion," but rather as the most extreme pro-abortion candidate to ever have run on a major party ticket.

He is the most extreme pro-abortion candidate ever to occupy the office of President of the United States. He was the most extreme pro-abortion member of the United States Senate. Indeed, he was the most extreme pro-abortion legislator ever to serve in either house of the United States Congress.

Yet there are Catholics and Evangelicals - even self-identified pro-life Catholics and Evangelicals - who aggressively promoted Obama's candidacy and even declared him to be the preferred candidate from the pro-life point of view.

What is going on here?

I have examined the arguments advanced by Obama's self-identified pro-life supporters, and they are spectacularly weak. It is nearly unfathomable to me that those advancing them can honestly believe what they are saying. But before proving my claims about Obama's abortion extremism, let me explain why I have described Obama as "pro-abortion" rather than "pro-choice."

According to the standard argument for the distinction between these labels, nobody is pro-abortion. Everybody would prefer a world without abortions. After all, what woman would deliberately get pregnant just to have an abortion? But given the world as it is, sometimes women find themselves with unplanned pregnancies at times in their lives when having a baby would present significant problems for them. So even if abortion is not medically required, it should be permitted, made as widely available as possible and, when necessary, paid for with taxpayers' money.

The defect in this argument can easily be brought into focus if we shift to the moral question that vexed an earlier generation of Americans: slavery. Many people at the time of the American Founding Fathers would have preferred a world without slavery but nonetheless opposed abolition. Such people ~ Thomas Jefferson was one, and Mrs. Abraham Lincoln was another, reasoned that given the world as it was, with slavery woven into the fabric of society, the economic consequences of abolition for society as a whole and in particular for owners of plantations and other businesses that relied on slave labor, would be dire.

Many people who argued in this way were not monsters, but honest and sincere, albeit profoundly mistaken. Some (though not Jefferson) showed their personal opposition to slavery by declining to own slaves themselves or freeing slaves whom they had purchased or inherited. They certainly didn't think anyone should be forced to own slaves. Still, they maintained that slavery should remain a legally permitted option and be given constitutional protection. General Grant was one such person, and he was also a slave owner.

Would we describe such people, not as pro-slavery, but as "pro-choice?" Of course we would not. It wouldn't matter to us that they were "personally opposed" to slavery, or that they wished that slavery were "unnecessary," or that they wouldn't dream of forcing anyone to own slaves. We would hoot at the faux sophistication of a placard that said "Against slavery? Don't own slaves!" We would observe that the fundamental divide is between people who believe that law and public policy should permit slavery, and those who think that owning slaves is an unjust choice that should be prohibited. Just for the sake of argument, though, let us assume that there could be a morally meaningful distinction between being "pro-abortion" and "pro-choice."

Who would qualify for the latter description? Barack Obama certainly would not. For, unlike his running mate Joe Biden, Obama does not think that abortion is a purely private choice that public authority should refrain from getting involved in.

If we stretch things to create a meaningful category called "pro-choice," then Biden might be a plausible candidate for the label; at least on occasions when he respects your choice or mine not to facilitate deliberate feticide. The same cannot be said for Barack Obama.

To begin with, he supported legislation that would have repealed the Hyde Amendment, which protects pro-life citizens from having to pay for abortions that are not necessary to save the life of the mother, and are not the result of rape or incest. The abortion industry laments that this longstanding Federal law, according to the pro-abortion group NARAL, "forces about half the women who would otherwise have abortions to carry unintended pregnancies to term and bear children against their wishes instead."

In other words, a whole lot of people who are alive today would have been exterminated in uteri were it not for the Hyde Amendment. Obama has promised to reverse the situation so that abortions that the industry complains are not happening (because the Federal Government is not subsidizing them) would happen.

That is why people who profit from abortion love Obama even more than they do his running mate.

But this barely scratches the surface of Obama's extremism. He has promised that "... the first thing I'd do as President is sign the Freedom of Choice Act" (known as FOCA). This proposed legislation would create a federally guaranteed "fundamental right" to abortion through all nine months of pregnancy, including, as Cardinal Justin Rigali of Philadelphia noted in a statement condemning the proposed Act, "a right to abort a fully developed child in the final weeks for undefined 'health' reasons."

In essence, FOCA would abolish virtually every existing state and federal limitation on abortion, including parental consent and notification laws for minors, State and Federal funding restrictions on abortion, and conscience protections for pro-life citizens working in the health-care industry - protections against being forced to participate in the practice of abortion or else lose their jobs. The pro-abortion National Organization for Women has proclaimed with approval that FOCA would "sweep away hundreds of anti-abortion laws (and) policies."

It gets worse. Obama, unlike even many "pro-choice" legislators, opposed the ban on partial-birth abortions when he served in the Illinois legislature and condemned the

Supreme Court decision that upheld legislation banning this heinous practice. He has referred to a baby conceived inadvertently by a young woman as a "punishment" that she should not endure. He has stated that women's equality requires access to abortion on demand.

Worse yet, he wished to strip federal funding from pro-life crisis pregnancy centers that provide alternatives to abortion for pregnant women in need. There is certainly nothing "pro-choice" about that.

But it gets even worse. Then Senator Obama, despite the urging of pro-life members of his own party, did not endorse or offer support for the Pregnant Women Support Act, the signature bill of Democrats for Life, meant to reduce abortions by providing assistance for women facing crisis pregnancies. In fact, Obama has opposed key provisions of the Act, including providing coverage of unborn children in the State Children's Health Insurance Program (S-CHIP), and informed consent for women about the effects of abortion and the gestational age of their child.

The legislation would not make a single abortion illegal. It simply sought to make it easier for pregnant women to make the choice not to abort their babies. The concrete test was whether Obama "pro-choice" rather than pro-abortion. He flunked. Even Senator Edward Kennedy voted to include coverage of unborn children in S-CHIP. But Barack Obama stood resolutely with the most stalwart abortion advocates in opposing it.

In an act of breathtaking injustice, which the Obama campaign lied about until critics produced documentary proof of what he had done, as an Illinois State Senator

Obama opposed legislation to protect children who are born alive, either as a result of an abortionist's unsuccessful effort to kill them in the womb, or by the deliberate delivery of the baby prior to viability. This legislation would not have banned any abortions.

Indeed, it included a specific provision ensuring that it did not affect abortion laws. (This is one of the points Obama and his campaign lied about until they were caught.) The Federal version of the bill passed unanimously in the United States Senate, winning the support of such ardent advocates of legal abortion as John Kerry and Barbara Boxer. But Barack Obama opposed it and worked to defeat it. For him, a child marked for abortion gets no protection (not even ordinary medical or comfort care) even if the baby is born alive and entirely separated from its mother. So Obama has favored protecting what is literally a form of infanticide.

You may be thinking it can't get worse than that. But it does.

For several years, Americans have been debating the use for biomedical research of embryos produced by in vitro fertilization (originally for reproductive purposes), but now left in a frozen condition in cryopreservation units. President Bush has restricted the use of Federal funds for stem-cell research of the type that makes use of these embryos and destroys them in the process.

Barack Obama, too, wants to lift the restriction. But Obama would not stop there. He co-sponsored a bill-strongly opposed by Senator John McCain - that would authorize the large-scale industrial production of human embryos for use in biomedical research in which they would be killed.

In fact, the bill Obama co-sponsored would effectively require the killing of human beings in the embryonic stage that were produced by cloning. It would make it a Federal crime for a woman to save an embryo by agreeing to have the tiny developing human being implanted in her womb so that he or she could be brought to term.

This "clone and kill" bill, if it were enacted, would have brought something to America that has heretofore existed only in China - the equivalent of legally mandated abortion. In an audacious act of deceit, Obama and his co-sponsors misleadingly called it an Anti-Cloning Bill. But it was nothing of the kind. What it bans is not cloning, but the embryonic children produced by cloning to survive. Can it get worse?

10

PRESIDENT OBAMA OPPOSED STEM CELL RESEARCH

D ecent people of every persuasion hold out the increasingly realistic hope of resolving the moral issue surrounding embryonic stem-cell research by developing methods to produce the exact equivalent of embryonic stem cells without using (or producing) embryos. But when a bill was introduced in the United States Senate to put a modest amount of Federal money into research to develop these methods, Barrack Obama was one of the few senators who opposed it.

From any rational vantage point, this is unconscionable. Why would someone not wish to find a method of producing the pluripotent cells scientists want that all Americans could enthusiastically endorse? Why create and kill human embryos when there are alternatives that do not require the taking of nascent human lives? It is as if Obama is opposed to stem-cell research unless it involves killing human embryos.

This ultimate manifestation of Obama's extremism brings us back to the puzzle of his pro-life Catholic and Evangelical apologists.

They typically do not deny the facts I have reported. But they cannot; each one is a matter of public record.

But despite Obama's injustices against the most vulnerable of human beings, and despite the extraordinary support he received from an industry that profits from killing the unborn (a good indicator of where he stands) some Obama supporters insist that he was the better candidate from the pro-life point of view.

They say that his economic and social policies would so diminish the demand for abortion that the overall number would actually go down — despite the Federal subsidizing of abortion and the elimination of hundreds of pro-life laws. The way to save lots of unborn babies, they say, was to vote for the pro-abortion - oops! "Pro-choice" candidate.

They tell us not to worry that Obama opposes the Hyde Amendment, the Mexico City Policy (against funding abortion abroad), parental consent and notification laws, conscience protections and the funding of alternatives to embryo-destructive research. They ask us to look past his support for Roe vs. Wade, the Freedom of Choice Act, partial-birth abortion, human cloning and embryo-killing. An Obama presidency, they insist, means less killing of the unborn.

This is delusional.

We know that the Federal and State pro-life laws and the policies that Obama promised to sweep away (and which John McCain said he would protect) save thousands of lives every year. Studies conducted by Professor Michael New and other social scientists have removed any doubt. Often enough, the abortion lobby itself confirms the truth of what these scholars have determined. Tom McClusky has observed that Planned Parenthood's own statistics show that in each of the seven states that have FOCA-type legislation on the books, "abortion rates have increased while the national rate has decreased."

In Maryland, where a bill similar to the one favored by Obama was enacted in 1991, he notes that "abortion rates have increased by 8 percent while the overall national abortion rate decreased by 9 percent." No one is really surprised. After all, the message clearly conveyed by policies such as those Obama favors is that abortion is a legitimate solution to the problem of unwanted pregnancies - so clearly legitimate that taxpayers should be forced to pay for it. But for a moment let's suppose, against all the evidence, that Obama's proposals would reduce the number of abortions, even while subsidizing the killing with taxpayer dollars. Even so, many more unborn human beings will likely be killed under the Obama presidency.

A Congress controlled by strong Democratic majority under Senator Harry Reid and House Representative Nancy Pelosi, plans to enact a bill authorizing the mass industrial production of human embryos by cloning for research using the aborted babies.

And President Obama will sign it. The number of tiny humans created and killed under this legislation (assuming that an efficient human cloning technique is soon perfected) could dwarf the number of lives saved as a result of the reduced demand for abortion - even if we take a delusionally - optimistic view of what that number would be.

Barack Obama and John McCain differ on many important issues about which reasonable people of goodwill, including pro-life Americans of every faith, disagree: how best to fight international terrorism, how to restore economic growth and prosperity, how to distribute the tax burden and reduce poverty, etc.

But on abortion and the industrial creation of embryos for destructive research, there is a profound difference of moral principle, not just prudence. These questions reveal the character and judgment of each man. Barack Obama is deeply committed to the belief that members of an entire class of human beings have no rights that have to be acknowledged and respected.

Across the spectrum of pro-life concerns for the unborn, he would deny the small and most vulnerable members of the human family the basic protection of the laws. Over the next four to eight years, as many as five or even six, U.S. Supreme Court justices will retire. Obama enthusiastically supports Roe vs. Wade and all indications are that given the opportunity as President, he will appoint judges who would support the morally and constitutionally disastrous decision and even expand its scope. Indeed, in an interview in Glamour magazine, he made it clear that he would apply a litmus test to Supreme Court nominations. Jurists who did not support Roe vs. Wade would not be considered for appointment.

John McCain, in contrast, opposes Roe vs. Wade and would appoint judges likely to overturn it. This would not make abortion illegal, but it would return the issue to the forums of democratic deliberation, where pro-life Americans could engage in a fair debate to persuade fellow citizens that killing the unborn is no way to address the problems of pregnant women in need of help.

What kind of America do we want our beloved nation to become?

Barack Obama's America is one in which being human, just isn't enough to warrant care and protection but an America where the unborn may legitimately be killed without legal restriction, even by the grisly practice of partial-birth abortion.

It is only in America where a baby that survives abortion, is not considered human, entitled to comfort care, as it lies struggling for life on a stainless steel table, or in a soiled linen bin. America is a nation in which some members of the human family are regarded as inferior and others superior in fundamental dignity and rights.

In Obama's America, public policy would make a mockery of the great constitutional principle of the equal protection before the law. By the way, the Constitution does not say that all men are equal, only that

"all men are equal before the law."

In perhaps the most telling comment made by any candidate in either party in an election year, then Senator Obama, when asked by Reporter Rick Warren when a baby gets human rights, replied:

"... that question is above my pay grade."

It was a profoundly disingenuous answer, for even at a state senator's pay grade, Obama presumed to answer that question with blind certainty. His unspoken answer then, as now, is chilling: human beings have no rights until infancy -- and if they are unwanted survivors of attempted abortions, not even then. But what of the medical doctors whose creed, whose Hippocratic Oath is to save lives? In America if a baby is still alive after it is aborted, it is not rushed to the Emergency Room of the nearest hospital; it is killed by other means. How inhuman. How cold-blooded! Is this not murder, and if not, why not? The stone-age Bushmen of the Kalahari are better than we Americans. The men stand between the lion seeking to attack their family, armed with nothing more than short spears and bows and arrows! These stone-age people would never hurt their babies!

In the end, the efforts of Obama's apologists to depict their man as the true pro-life candidate that Catholics and Evangelicals may and even should vote for, doesn't even amount to a nice try. Voting for the most extreme pro-abortion political candidate in American history is not the way to save unborn babies. It is a way to ensure their untimely death. I have added this article to my book because I think it has a lot of merit, even though some readers may not have a constitutional understanding that abortion is prohibited by the highest law of the land.

To sum up the abortion question:

> In the United States laws prohibiting abortion began to appear in the 1820s. Through the efforts primarily of physicians, the American Medical Association and legislators, most abortions in the U.S. had been outlawed by 1900. Illegal abortions were still done, though they became less frequent during the reign of the Comstock Law, which essentially banned birth control information and devices. Some early feminists, like Susan B. Anthony, wrote against abortion. They opposed abortion but only on the ground that at the time was an unsafe medical

procedure for women, endangering their health and life. Susan B. Anthony cared nothing about the unborn child or the U.S. Constitution.

These misnamed "feminists" believed that only the achievement of women's equality and freedom would end the need for abortion. Elizabeth Cady Stanton wrote in The Revolution:

> But where shall it be found, at least begin, if not in the complete enfranchisement and elevation of woman?

> They wrote that prevention was more important than punishment, and blamed circumstances, laws and the men they believed drove women to abortions.

Matilda Joslyn Gage, one of a few among the "feminists" who called abortion a crime, wrote in 1868:

> I hesitate not to assert that most of this crime of child murder, abortion, infanticide, lies at the door of the male sex...

Later feminists defended safe and effective birth control - when that became available — as another way to prevent abortion. (Most of today's abortion rights organizations also state that safe and effective birth control, adequate sex education, available health care and the ability to support children adequately are essentials to preventing the need for many abortions.)

What they all fail to mention is this cardinal fact: The most defenseless of us all, the unborn child in the womb, faces murder at the hand of the abortionist! Is this what they call "safe and effective?" What a sorry state of affairs! By 1965, all fifty states banned abortion, with some exceptions (which varied by state) to save the life of the mother, in cases of rape or incest, or if the fetus was deformed.

Groups like the National Abortion Rights Action League (NARL) and the Clergy Consultation Service (CCS) on Abortion worked to liberalize anti-abortion laws. The fact that the clergy had anything to do with the abortionists is another slap in the face of our Creator.

The Supreme Court in 1973, in the case of Roe vs. Wade, declared most existing state abortion laws unconstitutional. This decision is a fatal flaw in our legislative history because, as I have already explained herein, the Supreme Court is forbidden to legislate and under the 10th Amendment, cannot interfere in State law.

This decision ruled out any legislative interference in the first trimester of pregnancy and put limits on what restrictions could be passed on abortions in later stages of pregnancy. Roe vs. Wade, as I have amply demonstrated herein, is no law at all and therefore no State is bound to obey its fatally-flawed ruling especially as it can be forcefully argued that courts cannot legislate and that is what the Supreme Court did in the case of Roe vs. Wade.

While many celebrated the decision, others, especially in the Roman Catholic Church and in theologically conservative Christian groups, opposed the change. "Pro-life" and "pro-choice" evolved as the most common self-chosen names of the two movements, one to outlaw most abortions and the other to eliminate most legislative restrictions on abortions. Early opposition to the lifting of abortion restrictions included such organizations as the Eagle Forum, led by Phyllis Schlaffly, its president and founder. Today there are many national pro-life organizations which vary in their goals and strategies. Opposition to abortions has increasingly turned physical and even violent - first in the organized blocking of access to clinics which provided abortion services, organized primarily by Operation Rescue, founded in 1984 and led by Randall Terry. On Christmas Day, 1984, three abortion clinics were bombed, and those convicted called the bombings "a birthday gift for Jesus."

Within the churches and other groups opposing abortion, the issue of clinic protests has become increasingly controversial, as many who oppose abortions move to separate themselves from those who propose violence as an acceptable solution. The latest major conflict over abortion laws has been over termination of late pregnancies, termed "partial birth abortions."

Pro-choice advocates maintain that such abortions are to save the life or health of the mother or terminate pregnancies where the "fetus" cannot survive birth or cannot survive much after birth.

Pro-life advocates maintain that the "fetuses" may be saved and that many of these abortions are done in cases that aren't hopeless.

Here again we see extensive use of the word "fetus" when what should be said that it is a child in the womb or an unborn child. If the truth be known, most of the abortions performed in the U.S. are because the mother finds it inconvenient to have the baby and raise it like a normal mother would.

I maintain that when a woman agrees to an abortion in a non-life threatening situation, she has taken leave of her senses and should be adjudged "temporarily insane."

Abortion should be explained as euphemism for "murder by deception." For it is certain that to call a human baby a "fetus" is deception of the worst kind. Does a pregnant wife say to her husband, "I am pregnant; I am going to have your fetus!

Other titles

OMNIA VERITAS OMNIA VERITAS LTD PRESENTS:

DRUG WAR against AMERICA

The drug trade cannot be eradicated because its directors will not allow the world's most lucrative market to be taken away from them...

BY JOHN COLEMAN

The real promoters of this cursed trade are the "elites" of this world.

OMNIA VERITAS OMNIA VERITAS LTD PRESENTS:

FREEMASONRY from A to Z

In the 21st century, Freemasonry has become less a secret society than a "society of secrets".

by John Coleman

This book explains what masonry is

OMNIA VERITAS OMNIA VERITAS LTD PRESENTS:

THE ROTHSCHILD DYNASTY

by John Coleman

Historical events are often caused by a "hidden hand"...

OMNIA VERITAS
OMNIA VERITAS LTD PRESENTS:
ONE WORLD ORDER
SOCIALIST
DICTATORSHIP
All these years, while our attention was focused on the evils of communism in Moscow, the socialists in Washington were busy stealing from America!
BY JOHN COLEMAN
"The enemy in Washington is more to be feared than the enemy in Moscow."

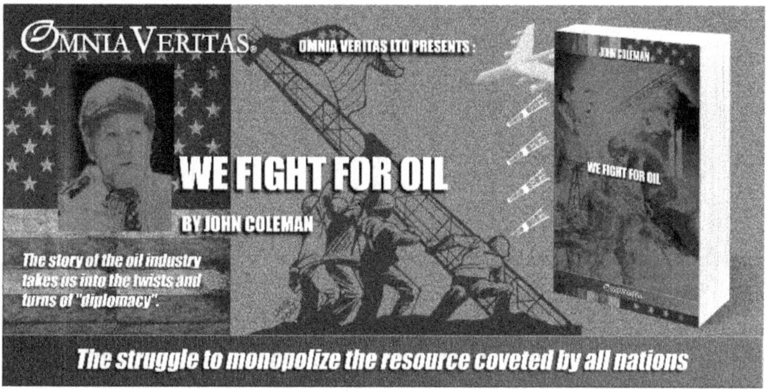
OMNIA VERITAS
OMNIA VERITAS LTD PRESENTS:
WE FIGHT FOR OIL
BY JOHN COLEMAN
The story of the oil industry takes us into the twists and turns of "diplomacy".
The struggle to monopolize the resource coveted by all nations

OMNIA VERITAS
Omnia Veritas Ltd presents:
THE SVALI CHRONICLES
BREAKING FREE FROM MIND CONTROL
TESTIMONY OF AN EX-ILLUMINATI
The Illuminati are a group of people who follow a philosophy known as "illuminism" or "enlightenment".
Understanding the programming of the Illuminati sect

The "Jewish mafia", that one, does not exist; the Western media do not talk about it...

The cynicism and malice of these conspirators is something beyond the imagination of most Americans.

Only one people bas irritated its host nations in every part of the civilized world

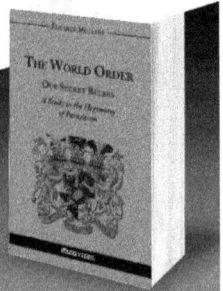

Printed in the USA
CPSIA information can be obtained
at www.ICGtesting.com
LVHW051534050124
767941LV00089B/4516

9 781805 401445